THE FATAL FLAW

JAMES R. WHITE

Crowne Publications, Inc.
P.O. Box 688
Southbridge, MA 01550

ISBN 0-925703-10-9

Printed in the United States of America

Acknowledgements

Many wonderful Christian people have helped to make this book a reality. First, Benny Diaz was instrumental in directing my thoughts toward Roman Catholicism, and his love for those in the Catholic Church is an inspiration to me. The loving people who make up Alpha and Omega Ministries cannot be thanked enough for their patience and support. Rich Pierce, Larry and Debby Vondra, Henry Wall, Rich Klaus, and Whitney Lynch have all helped in proofreading or just listening! My special thanks to D.L. for his support, and to my best friend, Jeff Niell, for his comments and criticisms as well. George and Aline Bonneau will never know how important their help has been. I also thank my Lord that He directed my family and I to a local church where God is glorified and the truth of the Word is held forth. To the pastor and people of the Phoenix Reformed Baptist Church I say "thank you" for being what God has called you to be, and for supporting me in this endeavor. And, as any married man knows, one simply cannot do one's best unless your wife is beside you. So, to my wonderful (and patient!) wife Kelli, thank you! "Who can find an excellent wife! Her worth far exceeds jewels! Many daughters have done well, but you excel them all!"

(Proverbs 30:10, 29).

In thankfulness to God I dedicate this book to my father, Edwin White. His patience and godliness has given me a foundation that is worth more than words can tell. I only hope I can be a father to my son as he has been to me.

James White
Phoenix, January 1990

Note: All translations of Scripture, unless otherwise indicated, are the author's own.

Table of Contents

Foreword

It is to be expected that a spirit of ecumenism prevails in these post Vatican II times. Both Roman Catholics and Protestants fail to understand the true nature of the Roman Catholic religion. Foundational dogmas are often ignored or blurred. False unity, charity and respectability are considered more important than the doctrine of Christ. Consequently, the majority fails to comprehend that modern Romanism is the same (even worse) as it was in the days of Luther and Melanchthon, Calvin and Farel. Rome hasn't changed her gospel; nor does she claim to have changed it. Her battle cry is "semper eadem!" — always the same. The Canons and Decrees of the Tridentine Council (1545 - 1563) which condemned justification by faith alone and the doctrine of a once-for-all sacrifice of Jesus Christ; which damn those who teach and believe the papacy. The Second Vatican Council (1962 - 1965) reaffirmed every Romish doctrine contested by the Reformers of the 16th century.

On the other hand, many of our Catholic friends fail

to understand the fundamentals of New Testament theology and the raison d'etre for the Protestant Reformation. Beseiged by traditional concepts and theories produced by medieval scholars on dogma and morality which claim to explain the Scripture text; fractured and splintered by the "new theologians" who want to revamp Catholicism from head to toe; thousands of sincere and pious souls are jettisoning the church of their birth. Even many of these are reexamining the Roman Catholic Church in the light of Holy Writ. As a former Roman Catholic priest, I have come upon thousands of ex-Catholics in this country and in other lands, now in agreement with the Reformers who held, "Quod non est Biblicum, non est theologicum" — what is not Biblical is not theological. Yet millions more are still enslaved by a false church proclaiming another gospel, a Christ dishonoring gospel.

One would expect any book written by a Protestant to explain the teachings of the Roman Catholic institution in relation to the Bible and Christianity, to be condemned by the religious hierarchy on the pretext that the author doesn't understand Roman Catholic doctrine. Sometimes this is true, but not with James R. White. He is scrupulous in measuring such ancient heresies as the sacrifice of the mass, purgatory, the atoning work of Christ and works-righteousness against the Scripture which "is quick, and powerful, and sharper than any twoedged sword, piercing even to the dividing asunder of soul and spirit, and of the joints and marrow, and is discerner of the thoughts and intents of the heart." Hebrews 4:12

The author is not a former Roman Catholic with an ax to grind against Catholicism, but a gracious theologian-apologist not looking to please men but God. THE FATAL FLAW is a positive testimony to one's faith. It has nothing to do with stubborn, stiff-necked resistance toward those who disagree with the author. Firm with the Scripture, tender and compassionate, he is willing to take the risk in offending people with apostolic truth because it's matter of life or death.

While I may differ somewhat with some of the particulars of this timely, urgent work, I heartily recommend its reading to any fair-minded person who isn't afraid to be sifted and tested. After all, truth has nothing to lose from an honest and candid discussion of the Scriptures. Jesus said, "And ye shall know the truth, and truth shall make you free." John 8:32

Bartholomew F. Brewer, Ph.D.
Founder/Director
Mission to Catholics International, Inc.
P.O. Box 19280
San Diego, CA 92119

Introduction

Allegiance to the Word of God produces, in the world's eyes, strange and radical results. One young man, on the road to success within his chosen career, abandoned it all and went out to become an itinerant preacher in a hostile and difficult world. He abandoned family, friends, and future for uncertainty and hardship. He did so because of his over-riding desire to be true to God's revelation, true to what he knew to be right. One expert on "destructive cults" with whom I happened to be speaking, when presented with this scenario, indicated that such a man would most likely be mentally deranged, and in need of counselling. The man was Saul of Tarsus, better known as the Apostle Paul.

There is a vast difference between *claiming* allegiance to the authority and accuracy of the Word of God, and *living* that way. There are many who claim some kind of reverence for, or obedience to, the Bible as the Word of God, but very, very few who *really* mean what they say. A large portion of "Christendom" in our modern world speaks highly of the Bible, while at the very same time denying its accuracy, its inspiration, and its final and total authority in any and all matters—whether doctrinal, historical or ethical. One cannot claim to be obedient to the Word when one is actually sitting in judgment of it by rejecting its authority and claims. But this is just what so many are doing today. Rejecting the authority of the Word, these men and women attempt to fit the words of Scripture into their own humanly-devised systems of thought, and the results are, unvaryingly, disastrous for the Gospel.

History tells us, however, that when men truly submit themselves to the authority of God's revelation, their lives can change the world. It was only a little over 400 years ago that certain men in Germany, France, Switzerland, England and elsewhere forever changed the face of the affairs of men when they refused to be subject any longer to human authorities and teachings, but rather determined to follow the Scriptures as their sole authority and guide. Historians have come up with a nearly unlimited number of theories to explain the strength of a Martin Luther or a John Calvin; an Ulrich Zwingli or a Theodore Beza. But the source of their power and perseverance seems obvious enough: these men were dedicated to the Word of God. They believed it was true, and its teachings were to be acted upon and trusted. They were not proud enough to stand in judgment of the Scriptures, but recognized their position as *created beings,* and hence in need of revelation from God, which they found in Scripture. Because of their obedience to the Word of God, they did and said things that, from a solely human point of view, were unwarranted, foolish, or downright silly. Luther spoke of men being saved *without* the works of the Roman Catholic system—how utterly outrageous! And Calvin spoke of God's absolute predestination of some to salvation, and others to damnation. Surely this is not how one becomes a popular leader! Why did they say such things? Because the Word of God taught these things! They were bound by conscience to teach and to believe that which the Bible presented to them as truth, and this they did.

Today each and every individual who names the name of Christ is faced with the same decision: will I own the Word of God as my authority, and do and say those things which I **know** it commands, even though this might result in personal hardship, even rejection, by others? Is my commitment to the Word of God, as the sole and sufficient source of all that is the Christian faith, stronger than my commitment to popularity and acceptance amongst that which is called "Christendom"? If we wish to have the same kind of effect upon our world that the Reformers had upon theirs, we must answer this question in all seriousness, and then act upon our decision.

It is here I find the main reason, the central compulsion, that causes me to write this book. It must be written, if I am to be consistent in my belief in, and dedication to, the Bible as the Word of God. Surely it would be far easier to address other issues. There are many "safe" topics that could be addressed. But if one is going to accept the clear and manifest teachings of the New Testament in regards to the nature of the Gospel, then one cannot sit quietly by while the doctrines of Romanism are presented more and more as being fully compatible with the Christian message.

When the Apostle Paul wrote to the churches in Galatia, he was obviously quite upset. For what reason? Why does this epistle contain some of the strongest language to be found in Scripture? Why does Paul place the teachers in Galatia under the **anathema** of God? From our modern perspective, it seems a little thing.

These teachers were not denying the importance of the work of Christ. Indeed, all they were saying was that faith in Christ was first, but after this one needed to observe certain aspects of the Mosaic Law, primarily circumcision. Surely this is not such a terrible thing! We have many today who are far more strident in their false teachings, going so far as to teach that God Himself was once a sinful man who lived on another planet! Now **there** is a sufficient reason for Paul to be upset, but why was he angered over such a small thing as the addition of something like circumcision to the Gospel message? Paul knew then what we must learn today: the Gospel is the power of God unto salvation. Any change in that Gospel message, then, leaves us not with a Gospel that is slightly in error, **but with no Gospel at all!** God saves in His way, not man's way, and to add man's works, no matter how minor they may seem to us, is to denigrate, no, *blaspheme*, the work of Christ! God is the one who saves. Therefore, to add human works to the process is to teach the very opposite of the truth. Since Paul loved the Galatian believers, he was more than willing to chastise them strongly for falling for such false teaching. It was their eternal salvation that was at stake.

One might call this kind of attitude in the Apostle "tough love" for it certainly was not easy for him to act or speak in such a way. Undoubtedly there were those in Galatia who commented, "My, what a mean-spirited person he is! How dare he speak in such a way!" Others probably wished to chide Paul for not being "loving" or "Christ-like" in his writing. But such folks don't understand the importance of the **truth** of the Gospel. They don't understand that love, real love, cannot be divorced from truth. One cannot claim to love when one is unconcerned about truth. The truth of the Gospel, then, must be the priority for one who really loves. So, Paul's letter, and his attitude, tells us what **love** *does* when faced with a dangerous falsehood. It reacts, and reacts strongly. It reacts in proportion to the danger presented, which here is eternal damnation itself.

Following Paul's example is rather unpopular these days. We live in an ecumenical age, where doctrinal distinctives are considered *passe*. The absolute authority of the Bible has been jettisoned by most major Protestant denominations, so the very concept of *truth* has become almost humorous. The fastest way to be labeled a "backward fundamentalist" is to let it slip that you think that there is actually **one** truth and that other positions are actually *in error!* But there is really little choice for the one who, by the working of God's Spirit, is led to bow to the truth and authority of the Word. Unpopular positions and statements are bound to be such a person's lot.

This book examines the "gospel" as presented by the Roman Catholic Church. It is this writer's position that the Roman system does not know the grace of God, nor the power of the completed and finished work of Jesus Christ. The "gospel" as presented by Rome, then, is not the Gospel taught in the New Testament. Rome has gone far beyond anything the Judaizers in Galatia ever dreamed of. If this be the case, then how can I betray the example given me by the New Testament and sit idly by while millions of Roman Catholics continue to think that what they have been taught will save them? And what of those many Christians who are being deceived into thinking that there *really isn't any difference* between Romanism and Christianity?

It is my belief that the greatest act of love I can show for those involved in Roman Catholicism is to warn them—loudly, clearly, and for as long as God wills—that any system that rejects the completed, finished, and utterly unique way of redemption in Jesus Christ is not going to save them. Such a system does not know God's power, and certainly does not have God's blessing. Full and complete salvation is to be found in Jesus Christ and in Him alone, not in a system that gives place to man's works and by so doing destroys the work of Christ, setting it at naught (Galatians 2:21). This is a wonderful message—a joyous message—that redemption *has been accomplished* once and for all in Jesus Christ! But before such *good news* can be accepted, *bad news* in the form of *false teachings* must be removed. This I shall seek to do in the following pages.

It is hoped that the reader, be he Protestant or Catholic, will consider carefully what is said here. May God bless you as you consider these things.

James White

Chapter 1
The Issues At Hand

It was the eve of the Reformation. The European societies had undergone great changes in the past two centuries. The Renaissance was in full swing, and notable advances in learning, due partially to the new availability of printed materials, were to be seen in every university in Europe. Literacy was on the rise. So, too, was nationalism. Germans were thinking of themselves more as Germans first than as members of the "Holy Roman Empire," and this was the case in many other nations as well. The power of the Roman Catholic Papacy had reached its zenith centuries before, and while the Pope still commanded great power, his prestige had been diminished in various ways. The memory of the "Great Schism" or the "Babylonian Captivity" of the Roman Church, during which time two (or at times three) rival Popes vied with one another for the supremacy, remained fresh in the people's minds. The monolithic claims of the See of Peter were marred by such historical embarrassments. Even more crippling was the well-known corruption within the church, not just amongst the priests (a very large portion of whom had secret wives and children) but all the way to the very top of the hierarchy. Popes of very recent memory had been famous for their extravagant life-styles and debauched behavior. This did little to help the Roman Catholic cause.

Funds for Papal projects were becoming more difficult to acquire. The Papal treasury, once fat with the income from various of the Roman Church's land holdings, was being pinched by the growth of a middle class that was not necessarily willing to see a large portion of its income going into Papal coffers. During the Middle Ages the Roman See had turned to the sale of indulgences as another form of revenue.[1] By 1517 the sale of indulgences had become an important aspect of European civilization, figuring prominently in the religious life of the people. An indulgence remitted the temporal punishment due for sin,[2] and it was popular belief for many that these indulgences also remitted the guilt or penalty of sin itself.[3] The belief in purgatory, where the souls of departed loved ones were undergoing torment to "purify" them before entering into heaven, was also widespread. Since these indulgences of the church were supposed to be able to aid these "poor souls" in purgatory and lessen their time there, many who lost loved ones were willing to spend large sums of money to help them out of their suffering. In Rome, the traffic in indulgences and the like was tremendous, with books circulating that claimed for their readers who would offer up the prayers they contained indulgences of as much as 11,000 years![4] Though many indulgences went to provide monies for local projects, a set percentage of all indulgences sold was to be sent to Rome.

Popes Julius II (1443-1513)[5] and Leo X (1475-1521) undertook the building of St. Peter's Basilica in Rome.

Such a project, of course, required tremendous sums of money, and Julius II announced a special indulgence to help raise the necessary funds. After the death of Julius, the matter was taken up by Leo X. Germany was at first spared from the selling of these new indulgences, but in 1517 this changed.[6] Albrecht (or Albert), who was elected archbishop of Mainz in 1514, had a vested interest in opening his area to the indulgence sellers, for it had cost him a total of **30,000 ducats** to buy his archbishopric, and the income from the indulgences (he would receive a percentage of the proceeds) would help him pay off the loans he had taken out to afford his position. Leo X, who would, of course benefit financially from Albrecht's actions, issued a bull in which was offered "complete absolution and remission of all sins" to those who would purchase the indulgence.[7]

This is how it came about that in 1517, one of Albrecht's underlings by the name of John Tetzel came into Saxony. Tetzel will forever be remembered as the "seller of indulgences," for it was he who gave impetus to Martin Luther's challenge of the selling of indulgences, made famous in Luther's "95 Theses". The text of one of Tetzel's indulgences follows:

> "May our Lord Jesus Christ have pity on thee, N.N., and absolve thee by the merits of his most holy passion! And I, in virtue of the apostolical power that has been confided to me, absolve thee from all ecclesiastical censures, judgments, and penalties, which thou mayest have committed, however great and enormous they may be, and from whatsoever cause, were they even reserved for our most holy father the pope and for the apostolic see. I blot out all the stains of inability and all

> marks of infamy that thou mayest have drawn upon thyself on this occasion. I remit the penalties that thou shouldst have endured in purgatory. I restore thee anew to participation in the sacraments of the Church. I incorporate thee afresh in the communion of saints, and re-establish thee in the purity and innocence which thou hadst at thy baptism. So that in the hour of death, the gate by which sinners enter the place of torments and punishment shall be closed against thee, and, on the contrary, the gate leading to the paradise of joy shall be open. And if thou shouldst not die for long years, this grace will remain unalterable until thy last hour shall arrive.
>
> "In the name of the Father, Son, and Holy Ghost. Amen.
>
> "Friar John Tetzel, commissary, has signed this with his own hand."[8]

The people of the land either took advantage of the indulgences, for various reasons, or hated them and those who sold them, for primarily nationalistic reasons. Germans did not like the idea of German gold going to Rome to build yet another monument in Italy.

Unknown to Tetzel, a certain Augustinian monk, and professor of theology at the University of Wittenberg, had been thinking and studying on the grace of God, and had come to conclusions that were directly opposite the concepts that made up the foundation of the entire system of indulgences. Martin Luther, a Roman Catholic priest and monk, had lived for years in search of peace with God. He did not find the rites, ceremonies, and sacraments of Romanism sufficient to convince him he stood in the proper relationship before a holy God. The holiness of God, that divine truth that has down through the ages grasped and pierced the hearts of godly men, frightened him, and filled him with dread. As a monk, Luther had spent as much as six hours in the confessional, trying desperately to fulfill what he had been taught were the requirements of God. Still he found no peace. He was sent to teach theology at the University of Wittenberg, and soon began to lecture on the Psalms. At about the same time, another of the pieces of the puzzle came together in the city of Basel. There, another Roman Catholic priest, Desiderius Erasmus, published the first printed edition of the Greek New Testament (1516). This was truly a momentous event, for one of these Greek New Testaments made its way into the hands of one Martin Luther in Wittenberg, who, upon completing his lectureship on the Psalms, moved on to Paul's epistle to the Romans.

As Luther struggled with the tremendous concepts put forth in Romans, he began to note the differences between the Latin *Vulgate* edition and the original Greek text. One of the most important differences had to do with the concept of repentance, something very close to the heart of Luther and his continuing struggle with sin and the judgment of God. The *Vulgate* rendered the Greek term *metanoia* into Latin as *paenitentiam agite*, "do penance." Yet, as he studied the Greek text, he realized that *metanoia* did not mean "do penance" but rather "repent, change one's mind." Having struggled with the fact that he *knew* that no amount of penances he performed gave him any freedom, any release, from the guilt of sin, this discovery in the text of the Scriptures was a keystone to his later thinking.

It was also at this time that Luther found, in that same book of Romans, the key to his prison, the answer to his quest. In reading the first chapter of Romans, he found, "But the just shall live by faith" (Romans 1:17). As Luther thought upon this verse, he began to see that a right standing with God is not based on penances, works, or anything else in man: righteousness comes by faith, and faith alone. His continued study of Romans only served to cement this conclusion, for this is the straight-forward argument of the entire book. When he cast himself upon God's mercy and grace, solely on the basis of his faith in the completed and finished work of Jesus Christ, and the promise of salvation that is to be found in Him, Luther experienced release from the bondage that had been his for so many years. Luther had been converted.

So, when it was reported to Luther that the Dominican Tetzel was selling indulgences and saying this and that about their effectiveness, Luther saw this teaching as a direct denial of the truths he himself was discovering in the Bible. Luther refused to allow any of those souls under his care in his parish to "get away with" indulgences; he told them they should repent and live a good life rather than trust in these little pieces of paper. When it got back to Tetzel that an Augustinian monk in Wittenberg refused to honor his indulgences, he reportedly was furious. There seemed little chance that Tetzel and Luther would not cross swords at some point.

Many historians mark the beginning of the Reformation at October 31, 1517, for it was on that day that Martin Luther nailed 95 propositions for debate on the subject of indulgences to the door (or possibly the door post) of the castle church at Wittenberg. Few today have read the "95 Theses" as they are called, and those who do are normally surprised that these articles, so often thought of as the beginning of Protestantism itself, are in fact very Roman Catholic in tone. But this should not be surprising, for Luther was at this point a loyal "son of the church." He had no intentions of leaving the

Roman Church, let alone being branded a "heretic." He simply did not believe that the sale of indulgences was in any way compatible with the teachings of Scripture, and, in the style of scholars, offered to debate anyone who thought they were. At this point Luther had not thought through the ramifications of his belief. But, having made the challenge, he would very soon have to think those things through, for his challenge was picked up by some anonymous benefactor, translated from Latin into German, and then printed, copies being distributed throughout Germany. Luther was an overnight hero for all those who opposed the indulgence trade. That had not been his desire or plan, but God had much more in the future for Martin.

Luther's challenge was taken up by one John Eck, well-known scholar and professor at Inglostadt. Eck published a tract in rebuttal of Luther entitled *Obelisks*, to which Luther replied with a tract entitled *Asterisk*. When Luther accompanied his friend Carlstadt (Luther's superior at Wittenberg) who was to debate Eck on "free will," Eck took the opportunity to turn the debate to Luther and his claims about indulgences. Having engaged the debate, Eck then skillfully turned the discussion to the question of authority, for indulgences were sold with the full approval and authority of the Pope; hence, to question the selling of indulgences was to question the very foundation of the Roman Catholic Church: the Pope. Luther replied with citations from the early church[9] and with Scripture. Eck then made it clear that Luther's position was parallel to the Bohemian priest John Hus, who had been burned for "heresy" over a century earlier at the Council of Constance (1414). At first Luther was taken aback by the claims of Eck, but, upon examining Hus' writings, admitted openly that much of what he had said was Christian and true. This was a very dangerous admission to make, for obvious reasons. Upon further review at a later date, Luther was to confess that he was a "Hussite," as were, he claimed, Augustine and Paul the Apostle.

Though Eck won the debate on a formal basis, he did much to lose the whole war, for his excellence in argument only served to make Luther think through his own position, and realize that he had to jettison the whole papal system if he was to believe what he found in Scripture about justification and redemption. Eck unknowingly sped up the process begun in Luther's study in Wittenberg.

The flame of Reformation spread. Luther was called before the Emperor, Charles V, and commanded to recant his beliefs. Luther, like Hus a century earlier, asked to be shown, from Scripture, where he had erred. He knew what was at stake. Not finding any evidence forthcoming from his inquisitors, and asked a final time to recant, Luther uttered these famous words:

> "Since your most serene majesty and your high mightiness require from me a clear, simple, and precise answer, I will give you one, and it is this: I cannot submit my faith either to the pope or to the councils, because it is clear as the day that they have frequently erred and contradicted each other. Unless therefore I am convinced by the testimony of Scripture, or by the clearest reasoning,—unless I am persuaded by means of the passages I have quoted,—and unless they thus render my conscience bound by the Word of God, I cannot and I will not retract, for it is unsafe for a Christian to speak against his conscience. Here I stand, I can do no other; God help me! Amen!"[10]

A conscience bound by the Word of God is a force that no pope, nation, or army can withstand. Within a few years of this famous confrontation between the German monk and the Emperor, Protestant cities and nations dotted the European map. Men like Ulrich Zwingli spearheaded the reform in Zurich; Martin Bucer in Strassbourg, and later John Calvin in Geneva. Men with a fearless faith like Daniel risked their lives to preach the Gospel as taught in Scripture.

As the Reformation grew stronger and stronger, and gained an ever widening sphere of influence, the Roman Catholic Church was forced to respond. Beginning in late 1545, a general council was held at the small town of Trent, in the Austrian Tyrol. While the *influence* of the Council of Trent has been enormous, as it truly shaped modern Roman Catholicism, and wrote in stone, so to speak, the dogmas of the Roman Church, in reality it was little more than a rubber-stamp party for the Pope. One writer records a common proverb of the day relating to the Council of Trent: "The synod was guided by the Holy Spirit, sent thither from time to time from Rome in a cloak-bag."[11] This referred to the fact that the papal representative basically "ran the show," introducing the Pope's agenda, and getting everyone's agreement. But, while the council itself might be less than awe-inspiring, the documents that came out of it defined Roman teaching for the next four centuries; and, in reference to the particulars of Roman Catholic theology in contrast with Protestant, those definitions remain in full force today.

As the Council of Trent ground out its various decrees, basically meeting for three periods of time between 1545 and 1564, they provided the classical statement of the Catholic faith. Along with their positive statements came lists of "canons," each providing an "anathema" (the curse of God) for anyone who would not believe as the synod instructed. The teachings of the Reformers, or at least caricatures of their beliefs, were obviously in the minds of the council members, for while not mentioning any of the Reformers by name, the doctrines presented by Luther on salvation,[12] Biblical authority, the sacraments, etc., were placed under the anathema.

To this very day, large segments of what might be called "conservative" or "traditional" Roman Catholicism look to the work of the Council of Trent as the expression of *the* truth *par excellence*. Indeed, some reject the more modern statements of Roman doctrine contained (primarily) in the decrees of the Vatican II council, claiming that that council contradicted the teachings of Trent. There can be no denial that modern Romanism, in all its many expressions, has been deeply influenced by, and in a great part molded by, the Council of Trent.

The rest of the history of the Reformation is well known: the fire begun could not be put out, and many of the nations of Europe were freed from the tyranny of the Roman system. This brief historical introduction sets the stage for understanding the issues that separated men like Martin Luther, Ulrich Zwingli, Martin Bucer, and John Calvin from the Roman Catholic system that had only fifty years earlier stood as the monolithic religious institution of Europe. What drove the Reformation? What were the theological issues? Are they relevant today? Why should anyone today care about the theological debates of monks who died centuries ago?

The Fundamental Issues

The story of Luther's break with the Roman system, and his reasons for doing so, provides for us a good outline of the fundamental differences between the teachings of Roman Catholicism, and the teachings of the Bible as re-discovered by Luther and the other Reformers. It began with the doctrine of salvation—how a man is made right with God. The Roman system presented a system of sacraments, through which the grace of God was dispensed to the individual. But this was all based upon the faithfulness and action of the person, and even when one had done all that could be done, there still was no assurance of full forgiveness. If a person followed all of the teachings of the Roman Church, there still remained the possibility (more of a *certainty*) of time in purgatory—maybe a *long* time—no one knew. The people were taught that one was joined to the Church by baptism; by this action one's sins were washed away. One was justified by this action, made right with God. But, any sin after baptism caused a stain to the soul—a venial sin would entail temporal punishment, but not the complete loss of justification, or "being in a state of grace." But a mortal sin would cause one to lose the grace of justification. Then one had to confess to a duly appointed priest, and receive forgiveness along with some kind of penance to perform. Or, one could also find forgiveness for one's venial sins through the "sacrifice of the Mass". The Mass was central to Roman Catholic dogma. The people were taught that each time the priest raised the host (the wafer-size piece of bread) above his head and gave the words of consecration, the bread and the wine in the cup would be turned into the body and blood of Jesus Christ, even while maintaining the "appearance"[13] of bread and wine. This Mass was said to be a *propitiatory* sacrifice that could remit sins—some of the theologians argued about fine points of whether it was the *guilt* of sin or the *penalty* of sin, or both, etc., but the person in the pew didn't follow most of that—they just knew that the Mass was supposed to be an unbloody sacrifice of Jesus. The Council of Trent expressed the belief at the time of the Reformation by stating,

> "And inasmuch as in this divine sacrifice which is celebrated in the mass is contained and immolated in an unbloody manner the same Christ who once offered Himself in a bloody manner on the altar of the cross, the holy council teaches that this is truly *propitiatory* and has this effect, that if we, contrite and penitent, draw nigh to God, we obtain mercy and find grace in seasonable aid. For, *appeased by this sacrifice*, the Lord grants the grace and gift of penitence and pardons even the gravest crimes and sins. For the victim is one and the same, the same now offering by the ministry of priests who then offered Himself on the cross, *the manner alone of offering being different.* The fruits of that bloody sacrifice, it is well understood, are received *most abundantly* through this unbloody one, so far is the latter from derogating in any way from the former. Wherefore, according to the tradition of the Apostles, it is rightly offered not only for the sins, punishments, satisfactions and other necessities of the faithful who are living, but also for those departed in Christ but not yet fully purified."[14]

Even after Mass, the hosts that were not used in the ceremony (only the priest drank the wine, the people were limited to taking the host or wafer) were kept in special containers. The faithful would then come and bow down before these pieces of the body of Christ, or at other times the priests would carry Christ around in procession, and people would stop and bow down in worship as the container went by.[15] But even here, a person could go to a thousand masses, and yet not have full assurance of missing purgatory, let alone facing the awful possibility that they might commit a mortal sin right before dying, and be lost forever. It was a continuous round of confession, penance, and more confession and penance.

On the other hand, the Reformers found a very different way in the New Testament. They were accused by the Catholics of "teaching a new gospel" and being under the condemnation of Galatians 1:6-9; and, if judged solely by what Rome was currently calling the "gospel," they were right—what the Reformers taught *was* new. But, as Luther and Zwingli and Calvin repeatedly affirmed, their gospel message was new *only because the Romanists had changed the original Gospel of Jesus Christ, substituting a man-centered system rather than the God-centered message of grace preached by the apostles*. Their gospel *was the same gospel* preached by Peter, Paul, John, and most of all, the Lord Jesus Himself.

The first distinctive of the Biblical Gospel over against the message taught by Rome was the role of God. Rather than God simply providing *a way of salvation,* the Reformers discovered that the Bible taught that God *actually saved men*. That is, rather than salvation being dependent upon *men's striving to take advantage of the plan made available by God,* the **real** Gospel taught that God was able to save men **independent** of any action on man's part. God, the Reformers taught, was absolutely **sovereign** in the matter of salvation. He had, from time immemorial, chosen, elected, predestined to save certain men and bring them into fellowship with Himself, and, since God will never fail to do that which He purposes, those whom God has chosen *will be saved!* Rather than a man-centered message that made the operative factor man and man's will and decisions, the Bible presented a God-centered message in line with the words of the Psalmist, "Our God is in heaven; He does whatever pleases Him" (Psalm 115:3).

Next, the Reformers found that the Biblical teaching about man was very different than the elaborate system worked out by medieval theologians such as Thomas Aquinas. They found that sin had affected *all of man,* to the point that Paul could say, "There is none righteous, there is none who understands, there is not one who seeks after God" (Romans 3:10-11). This meant that even man's will was enslaved to evil, *incapable of seeking* after God or doing right. Outside of the sovereign work of God by the Holy Spirit, man was utterly helpless to even *will* to be saved, let alone *be saved* through whatever system of works, ceremonies, penances, etc. that might be presented. "And you, **being dead in your transgressions...**" (Eph. 2:1) is how the Apostle expressed it. Dead in sin, not just wounded by sin, deprived of some original righteousness by sin, hindered by sin. This was a radical concept in that day, for it clearly meant that all the "aids" or "helps" that could possibly be concocted would be of no avail to someone who is **dead!** No amount of sacraments could help a dead person—God had to act first to bring spiritual life. This also meant that faith and repentance *had to be gifts of God*, for they were not within the ability of sinful man.

Martin Luther spoke and wrote much about the eternal predestination of men to salvation by God. But, by a twist of history, his name is not normally associated with the doctrine of predestination.[16] Rather, that honor has fallen to the French theologian and pastor of the Church at Geneva, John Calvin. Calvin's scholarly, eminently Biblical, and (for some frustratingly) logical presentation of the doctrine has become **the** classic expression of the doctrine. The Reformer taught that God, in His mercy and love, did, solely and completely on the basis of His own holy will, choose, elect, and predestine certain men unto salvation. His choice *was not in any way, shape, or form based upon any action of man.* No man deserved salvation in the first place; God's choosing *any* was an act of incomprehensible grace. While the Roman system acknowledged the *term* "predestination" (anyone who read two pages of Augustine had to reckon with his teaching on the subject), the strength, beauty, grace, and reality in every day life, had been stripped away through the emphasis upon man's will, man's actions, man's decisions. But as the Reformers read such passages as Romans chapter 9, Ephesians chapter 1, or John chapter 6, they saw how clearly and forcefully the Bible presented God's eternal and unalterable predestination. And, typically for these men of God, they saw this for what it was: an awesome expression of God's love, mercy, and above all, His tremendous grace.

The work of Jesus Christ was again seen, as it was presented in Scripture, as God's sole and only way of salvation. But, beyond this, it was just as surely seen to be a *completed, finished, and, most importantly, an already applied work.* The Reformers denied that Christ is sacrificed (in an unbloody manner) in the Mass; for they saw that this would mean that Christ's sacrifice on the Cross of Calvary in and of itself was incomplete. Propitiation, redemption, reconciliation—all of this was accomplished in the one sacrifice of Christ, and there simply was no need for that work to be represented, re-enacted, renewed in the Mass. Since the elect of God died with Christ, and that work was applied to each individual member of the elect at the point of regeneration (which was *not* at baptism), why should Christ be made present again and again upon the altar of Roman churches? No, as the writer to the Hebrews said, Christ entered into the holy place "*having obtained eternal redemption*" (Heb. 9:12). Christ did not win for God's people a *theoretical or contingent salvation*, but a **real and finished** one.

Since this was so, then God's choosing of an individual could not fail but bring about His intended result of salvation. The "irresistible grace" of God would draw each and every man and woman who was the object of God's mercy and grace infallibly to Christ, just as Jesus had said in John 6:37, "All that the Father gives Me shall come to Me." In a world where most dreaded the indeterminate amount of time they would almost surely spend in purgatory, suffering for their sins, the idea of God's surely saving a man, imputing to him the righteousness of Jesus Christ, and bringing him at death directly into His presence was a radical message indeed. "Presumptuous!" cried the Roman Catholic. "The Gospel!" responded the Christian, who went on to assert that the Catholic position made the work of Christ, and the will of God, dependent upon man's works and actions, and hence rendered them ineffective, impotent to bring about the salvation of even one individual outside of man's assistance.

Such beliefs could not exist *within* the Roman Catholic system, as Luther quickly discovered. The selling of indulgences by John Tetzel contradicted everything Luther was finding the New Testament taught; yet, Tetzel was doing what he was doing with the Pope's blessing and approval. How could the man who people believed was the "Vicar of Christ on earth"[17] allow such an anti-Biblical activity to go on, unless, of course, he actually *was not* the Vicar of Christ? And so Luther began to question the doctrine of the papacy and the infallible teaching authority of the Pope. He quickly discovered that the form of government of the New Testament Church was radically different than the complex hierarchical form found in Rome, and he further discovered that the passages utilized by Roman Catholic theologians (such as himself until he began looking to Scripture as his authority) did not support the system that resulted from their claims. Further, the Roman Church claimed that no one could hold a position other than the one defined by the papacy. History was littered with the burnt bodies of those who tested the resolve of the Roman hierarchy to maintain their absolute control over theology and belief. Luther was vividly reminded of this by Eck when the subject of the teachings of Hus was broached in the Leipzig debate. Indeed, the story is told of Luther's going to Worms to meet with the Emperor in 1521. Just as Hus before him, Luther was given a promise of "safe passage" by the Emperor; that is, the Emperor promised that Luther could come to Worms and go back home without fear of being harmed. Hus had trusted a similar promise, but had been arrested and burned for refusing to recant his "heresies" which Luther was now preaching. As Luther came into Worms, it is said, scrawled on a wall of the city was the warning: "LUTHER: THE SAXON HUS!" Standing for one's beliefs, when those beliefs were considered by a man in Rome to be wrong, was a far different matter then than it is for most believers today.

Hence, for the Reformers to be faithful to what they found plainly taught in Scripture required that they break completely with the Roman system. Rome did not preach the same gospel, did not have the same authority. And, as they broke more and more from the traditions of Romanism, they began to see that *a very large portion* of the popular piety of the day—veneration of images, saints, prayers to Mary, etc.—were not only *non-Biblical*, but **anti-Biblical**, forbidden to believers by the Word of God. They concluded that one had a choice to make: one either believed what the Bible said, or one remained a Roman Catholic. There simply was no way to do both. Faith in Christ, they felt, demanded a repudiation of the Pope who claimed to be the Lord's substitute on earth.

And today...

The reader will hopefully forgive me the historical digression. I recognize that history is not the greatest interest of most modern people, whether Protestant or Roman Catholic. But this is to our hurt, not our benefit, for the issues faced by Luther or Zwingli simply have not gone away. They face each and every person who would claim the name "Christian" whether they wish to acknowledge their presence or not. Sadly, today, most continue on in blissful ignorance of the *absolute necessity* of facing, and answering, the questions that the Reformers were brave enough to answer. If you continue on in reading this book, you too will have to answer hard questions about what is, and what is not, Christian doctrine and teaching.

We live in an age of "ecumenism." Everywhere we look, we find "dialogue" going on between Catholic and Protestant. I have nothing against "dialogue" in and of itself, but it seems that the vast majority of these dialogues are not based upon any desire to present the truth of God, as found in Scripture, but rather to find areas of agreement at the expense of doctrinal distinctives. These discussions, if they are to have any validity for a Christian at all, must first of all define the key issues of the Gospel, and assert that any issue discussed must be related first and foremost to that truth.

One who takes the New Testament as authoritative must realize that for any *real* unity to exist between Christians, *it must* exist upon the only ground that true Christian unity can be based: the unadulterated truth of the Gospel of Jesus Christ. *Any discussion, action, or coalition that does not have as its primary design the propagation of the true Gospel of Jesus Christ must, by definition, be foreign to the Christian Church.* It is simply **impossible** to claim faith in Jesus Christ and yet be unconcerned about the message of His Cross.

Could "ecumenical" dialogue, then, properly take place with the Roman Catholic Church? In our opinion, no, it cannot. Why? That is the subject of this book. Some books make you hunt and search or make a wild guess about the "thesis statement"; We shall be quite open about it. Here it is: **The Roman Catholic Church's teaching on the work of Jesus Christ (specifically, His atonement) is anti-Biblical and false; hence, the Roman Catholic Church is not in possession of the Gospel of Jesus Christ, and cannot, therefore, be considered a Christian church.** Therefore, not only would ecumenical dialogue be an impossibility, but the Christian Church must make the evangelization of Roman Catholics a great priority.

It is our contention that the *fatal flaw* of Roman Catholic theology is to be found in its false teaching on the work of Jesus Christ on the cross of Calvary. To the end of demonstrating the truth of this contention, we will very carefully document the position of the Roman Church on two subjects that best illustrate their teaching: the "sacrifice of the Mass" and the teaching of purgatory. In so doing, we will demonstrate that *the Roman Catholic Church presents ways and means outside of the completed work of Jesus Christ whereby sin (either in reference to its guilt or its punishment) is atoned or propitiated.* This fact, if demonstrated, is more than sufficient to forever ban such teaching from the title "Christian."

A word should be said about the extent of the documentation from Roman Catholic sources. It is our intention to quote *numerous* Roman Catholic sources in demonstrating the position of Rome on the issues to be examined in this work. We will draw heavily from the official decrees of the Council of Trent as well as the documents of Vatican II. Various catechisms and works of theology will also be referenced, some from the "conservative" side, some from the more modern. We feel it is vital to be very careful in documenting *anyone's* position with which we are to disagree. There simply is no benefit, and no reason, for misrepresenting the Catholic position. We will at times go *beyond* what would be necessary to *make sure* that the Catholic position is understood and accurately portrayed. Nothing bothers us more than to be misrepresented in a debate; therefore, to be consistent, we must be careful to accurately present the position against which we are arguing. "Straw men" are easy to create, and easier to knock down. There are, sad to say, far too many "anti-Catholic" books and works around that show little or no concern for accurate citation or presentation. We know that it is impossible for us to make every Catholic happy with our presentation of Catholic beliefs, for Romanism presents a rather multi-form spectrum of perspectives in our modern day. But we will stick with the published works of the RCC[18] in defining terms, beliefs, doctrines, etc. That will not mean, of course, that we agree with those definitions, beliefs, or doctrines—but, if the Roman position is clearly presented, we will be able to contrast the Biblical teaching that much more clearly and forcefully.

If you are reading this book expecting it to be a "Catholic bashing party," you will be sorely disappointed. We have no desire to "bash Catholics." The author is primarily an apologist and theologian, and his heart's desire is that each person reading this might be confronted with the Bible's magnificent proclamation of the finished work of Jesus Christ in His atonement. For the Roman Catholic, this would mean a liberation from the false concepts embodied in the Mass and purgatory. Nothing would please us more than if our blessed Lord used these words to free Catholics from their bondage to a system that does not bring to them the "power of God" in the real Gospel. If you are a Catholic, and you associate us for any reason with those who would attack your faith and beliefs for no other reason than simply the joy of debate, then allow us to ask you to lay aside your prejudices, even if they are derived from reading "anti-Catholic" materials that are, quite clearly, far from meeting the standards of Biblical integrity and truthfulness. Take the time to weigh our words, and consider the divine revelation of God in Scripture.

Furthermore, a word of warning should be presented for the non-Catholic reader of this work. If you are a Christian, the chances are *great* that you will be challenged by what will be said about the work of Christ in this book as well. The sad fact of the matter is, *a large majority of modern "Protestantism" has embraced concepts in regards to the work of Christ, and all of salvation in general, that do not come from the Reformers, but from Catholicism itself!* Modern "evangelicals" are quick to place the final decision in regards to salvation in the hands of man; the atonement of Christ, for the vast majority of modern Christians, is universal in scope; that is, Christ died for everyone, yet, in dying, He really didn't save anyone, since the decision is up to us. Just as Romanism was, at the time of the Reformation, and remains today, man-centered in its doctrine of salvation, so too is modern evangelicalism.[19] The great

Biblical doctrines of God's sovereignty, man's inability, the definite, specific work of Jesus Christ on behalf of His people, God's efficacious and effective grace, and the perseverance of the saints in holiness, are rarely heard from modern Protestant pulpits.[20] If you are an evangelical Christian who believes in the authority and inspiration of Scripture, and agrees with us that the Bible and the Bible alone is the sufficient and sole rule of faith, then it is *to you* that we say: read closely; consider what is said. *Have you accepted concepts and ideas that are more closely allied to the Roman position than with the Bible?* If so, are you willing to continue to read, to pray, to study, and find out if the *very popular* concepts presented in much of Christian radio, television, and books are *really* the truth? You may have wondered why the Christian Church seems to make so few inroads into the Roman Catholic community. May we suggest an answer? *We believe that modern evangelicalism has little to say to Roman Catholicism, since it agrees with Rome on some of the most basic issues of the Gospel!* Go back to the Reformers who had to deal with Romanism each and every day and you will *not find* them saying what most TV preachers say today![21] The Reformers' method was centered on God and His glory; their message was Jesus Christ and Him crucified. Man was seen as guilty before God, utterly helpless to do anything but to cry to God for mercy, trusting in the complete and sufficient work of the Lord Jesus, not in any action of their own. Is the modern evangelical message the same? Look at some of the tracts in your Bible or in the glove compartment of your car. What is the central aspect of the tract? Is it man? Is the final decision man's? Is it said that God *has saved* in Christ Jesus, or that He *might save* **if man decides to let him?** The Reformers could speak to Roman Catholics because their message differed from Roman belief at the most basic levels. Modern evangelicalism, having abandoned its historical roots, has moved back onto the same ground as Romanism, leaving it with little basis to decry the falsehoods taught by the Pope in Rome.

The view that is presented in this work is unashamedly Reformed. Hence, just about *everyone* reading this book will be challenged to think through their position. That is our intent. In our opinion, works that do not challenge the reader are rarely worth the time to read. Roman Catholics will be challenged at nearly every turn; modern evangelicals just a little less often. May God guide us all as we examine His infallible Word.

Chapter 2
The Roman Catholic Doctrine of Salvation

Before one can properly appreciate and understand the central role of the Mass in Roman Catholic theology, one must at least have a basic grasp of a few of the other concepts touching the doctrine of salvation. It is not our intention to be exhaustive in reviewing each and every aspect of these doctrines; they are presented so that the reader, especially the non-Catholic, will have a basis of understanding from which the much fuller discussion of the Mass and purgatory can be launched. The Biblical perspective on many of these issues will be presented at a later time.

The Roman Catholic Church claims to be the continuation of the Church founded by the Lord Jesus Christ nearly two millennia ago. The authority given by Jesus Christ to the Apostles, and primarily to Peter, has, according to the RCC, been passed down in unbroken succession to this very day. This teaching authority of the church, we are told, is the basis of the RCC's claim to sole proprietorship over the interpretation of the text of Scripture. The Council of Trent, for example, more than once condemns those who would interpret the

Bible in any way other than that provided for in the Council's decisions.[1] It is not necessary here to go into the whole discussion of Scripture and authority,[2] only to note that Romanism bases its teachings in regards to salvation *not on the Bible alone, but on the Bible interpreted by their own authority, coupled with a further "source" or "mode" of revelation, that being "sacred tradition."*

Three basic areas of discussion will serve to present the Roman perspective on salvation: the nature of sin, justification, and the sacraments. Most of the necessary aspects of the doctrinal stance of Rome can be presented under these three heads.

The Nature of Sin

It is primarily the *definition* of sin that is important in understanding Roman teaching. The basic concepts of sin being rebellion against God and God's law are not disputed. Neither is it contested that sin separates man from God, though the *extent* of the separation, and the results for the "natural" or lost man is an issue of disagreement. The important issue here, however, revolves around the *kinds* of sin, and the *penalties* of sin, along with just *how* sin is forgiven.

Roman Catholicism separates sin into two major categories: venial and mortal. Roman Catholic theologian John Hardon defines venial sin:

> "An offense against God which does not deprive the sinner of sanctifying grace. It is called venial (from *venia*, pardon) because the soul still has the vital principle that allows a cure from within, similar to the healing of a sick or diseased body whose source of animation (the soul) is still present to restore the ailing bodily

function to health."[3]

On the other hand, mortal sin is:

> "An actual sin that destroys sanctifying grace and causes the supernatural death of the soul. Mortal sin is a turning away from God because of a seriously inordinate adherence to creatures that causes grave injury to a person's rational nature and to the social order, and deprives the sinner of a right to heaven."[4]

A person enters into a state of "sanctifying grace" through baptism at the hands of the Roman Church.[5] So it is seen that venial sins, "daily sins" as they are often called, do not destroy sanctifying grace, but impede spiritual progress. It is not even necessary to confess venial sins in the sacrament of confession to the priest,[6] but these can be "expiated" by means of "sorrow, prayer, works of charity and abstinence, reception of Holy Communion..."[7] There is no clear and infallible guide as to just what is, and what is not, venial sin; and the line between venial and mortal sin is difficult to trace with absolute certainty from Roman writings. Mortal sins destroy sanctifying grace, and, unless they are confessed, bar one from entering into heaven.[8]

When a Roman Catholic confesses to the priest, the priest (by his power of ordination, coming to him through the church[9]) absolves the penitent person of the *guilt* and the *eternal punishment* of the sin; however, he does *not* necessarily remove the "temporal punishment" of the sin. Rather, he assigns works of penance or contrition, *by which the person then provides "satisfaction" for his sins, thereby removing the penalty.* This is a vital point, hence it should be fully understood:

> "Finally, in regard to satisfaction... the holy council declares that it is absolutely false and contrary to the word of God, that the guilt is never remitted by the Lord without the entire punishment being remitted also... And it is in keeping with divine clemency that sins be not thus pardoned us without any satisfaction... Neither was there ever in the Church of God any way held more certain to ward off impending chastisement by the Lord than that men perform with true sorrow of mind these works of penance. Add to this, that while we by making satisfaction suffer for our sins, we are made conformable to Christ Jesus who satisfied for our sins, from whom is all our sufficiency... Neither is this satisfaction which we discharge for our sins so our own as not to be through Christ Jesus; for we who can do nothing of ourselves as of ourselves, can do all things with the cooperation of Him who strengthens us...no Catholic ever understood that through our satisfactions the efficacy of the merit and satisfaction of our Lord Jesus Christ is either obscured or in any way diminished."[10]

The claim that the concept of satisfaction does not diminish from the satisfaction derived from the work of Christ will be dealt with in its place; for now, it is clear, this claim is not in harmony with Biblical teaching. Another Roman theologian notes,

> "All temporal punishments for sin are

> not always remitted by God with the guilt of sin and the eternal punishment."[11]

In Roman Catholic theology, there is a difference between *guilt* and *temporal punishment* of sin. The work of Christ, applied by the "laver of regeneration" (i.e., baptism)[12] cleanses from the guilt of sin (including original sin) and results in justification.[13] However, as Trent explains,

> "If anyone says that after the reception of the grace of justification the guilt is so remitted and the debt of eternal punishment so blotted out to every repentant sinner, that no debt of temporal punishment remains to be discharged either in this world or in purgatory before the gates of heaven can be opened, let him be anathema."[14]

According to Trent, the temporal punishments of sins *committed before baptism* are remitted by baptism; but, if one sins *after* baptism, even when these sins are forgiven through the sacrament of confession, the *temporal punishments* remain.[15] And these punishments are "expiated" by men's works either in this life, or, if a person dies with unexpiated punishments remaining, in purgatory, there to be satisfied by suffering. Hence, men's actions, including suffering, tears, prayers, pilgrimages, acts of charity, etc., are considered in Romanism to *have merit* in God's eyes. As one writer puts it,

> "By his good works the justified man really acquires a claim to supernatural reward from God."[16]

Another wrote,

> "Man, for his part, in order to arrive at full sanctification, must cooperate with the grace of the Holy Spirit through faith, hope, love of God and neighbor, and prayer;[17] but he must also perform other "works." It is a universally accepted dogma of the Catholic Church that man, in union with the grace of the Holy Spirit must merit heaven by his good works. These works are meritorious only when they are performed in the *state of grace* and with a *good intention*... We have shown that according to Holy Scripture the Christian can actually merit heaven for himself by his good works."[18]

So, "good works" are meritorious, not only positively in regards to earning eternal life, but negatively in making "satisfaction" before God in expiating one's sins, specifically the temporal punishment due those sins. It is only fair to remember that Roman Catholic theologians are always very careful to assert that these concepts of satisfaction, merit, good works, etc., do not in any way detract from the satisfaction, merit, and work of Jesus Christ. This is the Roman claim. Whether it can withstand a Biblical or logical examination is a very different issue.

In conclusion, remember that according to the RCC sin is of two kinds: venial and mortal, the first not resulting in eternal punishment, but the second causing eternal separation from God. It should also be emphasized that a sin can be *forgiven* in Roman theology, yet there might be *punishment* remaining, even after the sin is forgiven. This will become *very* important in discussing the atonement of Christ, His work of redemption.

Justification

The Reformers rightly emphasized the Biblical term *justification*. They preached that justification was by faith *alone*, or, as they put it, *sola fide*. Forced to respond to this constant emphasis in Reformed proclamation, the Council of Trent early on addressed the doctrine of justification. The decree contained 16 chapters and 33 canons condemning various teachings, including, of course, those presented by the Reformers. The decree opened,

> "Since there is being disseminated at this time, not without the loss of many souls and grievous detriment to the unity of the Church, a certain erroneous doctrine concerning justification...the holy, ecumenical, and general Council of Trent...to expound to all the faithful of Christ the true and salutary doctrine of justification...strictly forbidding that anyone henceforth presume to believe, preach or teach otherwise than is defined and declared in the present decree."[19]

The Council continues by asserting that though Christ died for all, "yet all do not receive the benefit of His death, but those only to whom the merit of His passion is communicated"[20] which is "effected... through the laver of regeneration..." that is, by baptism.[21] It then asserts that God gives "predisposing grace" to the individual that is in no way "merited" by anyone; yet, it continues on to say that they "may be disposed through

His quickening and helping grace to convert themselves to their own justification by freely assenting to and cooperating with that grace..."[22] Next, repentance is said to be a necessary action. After all of this "preparation" one is finally justified:

> "This disposition or preparation is followed by justification itself, which is not only a remission of sins but also the sanctification and renewal of the inward man through the voluntary reception of the grace and gifts whereby an unjust man becomes just and from being an enemy becomes a friend...the instrumental cause is the sacrament of baptism, which is the sacrament of faith, without which no man was ever justified finally...Wherefore, when receiving true and Christian justice, they are commanded, immediately on being born again, to preserve it pure and spotless, as the first robe given them through Christ Jesus in place of that which Adam by his disobedience lost for himself and for us, so that they may bear it before the tribunal of our Lord Jesus Christ and may have life eternal."[23]

This definition of justification, however, should be carefully distinguished from what many Protestant readers would understand as justification. The Roman concept of "being justified" is hardly permanent, for it can be "undone" by the commission of a mortal sin. It is, in the clearest sense of the term, a "conditional" justification, one that is not permanent, but is dependent upon the continued faithfulness of the person. The "incompleteness" of this justification can be seen in the fact that in Chapter 10 of this decree it is asserted that one can "increase" in justification: "through the observance of the commandments of God and of the Church, faith cooperating with good works, increase in that justice received through the grace of Christ and are further justified..."[24] Various denials of Reformed (and we might point out, Biblical) doctrines are put forth: a denial of justification by faith and faith alone follows quickly. Indeed, in summing up the matter, it is claimed that a person *cannot be justified* without accepting the definitions just put forward by the Council.[25] In the canons that follow, anyone who would present Paul's doctrine of the bondage of the will (Romans 3:11) is placed under the anathema (by Canons 4 and 5); anyone accepting the truth of Romans 3:28 that justification comes by faith alone, is cursed by Canons 9, 12, and 14. Eternal predestination is anathematized in Canon 17; the concept that good works flow *from* justification, but are not the *cause* of its increase is condemned by Canon 24; belief that the forgiveness of sins *includes* the punishment is banished by Canon 30; any who would reject the idea of merit being attached to works is condemned by Canon 32; and finally, anyone who would assert that the Roman Catholic doctrine on justification "derogates in some respect from the glory of God or the merits of our Lord Jesus Christ...let him be anathema" (Canon 33).

The Sacraments

What is a sacrament? Roman Catholic John O'Brien answers:

> "[Christ] likewise established the sacraments which serve as so many channels through which the graces and bless-

> ings of the Redemption reach the soul of each individual recipient. The administration of the sacraments was entrusted to the Church to which Christ gave complete jurisdiction over the deposit of divine truth and over the means of sanctification. In a very true sense the Church may be said to be the extension of the Incarnation...A sacrament is an outward sign of inward grace...The sacraments and the holy Sacrifice of the Mass are the chief channels through which the fruits of the Redemption, the blessings and graces of God, are applied to individual souls...Christ by His suffering and death gained vast spiritual riches for us; they may be said to constitute a huge spiritual reservoir. It is necessary that some means be devised to tap the reservoir and carry its riches to our souls. The sacraments are such means: channels of divine grace to the souls of men."[26]

Sacraments, then, are "channels of grace," the means by which the grace of God is applied to individual men. According to modern Roman teaching, the sacraments number seven: Baptism, Confession, Holy Eucharist, Confirmation, Holy Orders, Matrimony, and Extreme Unction. We have already seen that the sacrament of Baptism forgives sins; it "makes us heirs of heaven and co-heirs with Jesus Christ."[27] It is said to unite us with Christ, to make us a part of the body of Christ.[28] Baptism is an absolute necessity for salvation, for as Canon 5 of the *"Decree Concerning the Sacraments"* from Trent says, "If anyone says that baptism is optional, that is, not necessary for salvation, let him be anathema."[29] And, if one disagrees with this view of baptism, one is condemned by anathema as well (Canon 3).

The other two sacraments that bear directly on the discussion of salvation are Confession and Holy Eucharist. The Eucharist will take up our attention in the next chapter. Confession has been alluded to already in our discussion of sin and justification. Ott provides a brief definition:

> "The Sacrament of Penance...is that Sacrament by which the sinner, who repents of his sins, acknowledges them sincerely and has the will to render atonement, has his sins, committed after his Baptism, remitted in the absolution pronounced by the priest. The word penance is also used to designate a particular part of the Sacrament of Penance, i.e., the satisfaction."[30]

The sacrament is made up of three parts: contrition, confession, and satisfaction. Contrition is the sorrow for sin; confession the action of confessing those sins to the priest to receive absolution for them (an action which is absolutely necessary for salvation for anyone who would commit a mortal sin after their baptism);[31] satisfaction is undergoing some kind of penance, normally assigned by the priest, to expiate the temporal punishment for the sin(s).

The Reformers rejected the concept of penance, confession, and satisfaction, because all of these, they felt, in one way or another denied the sufficiency of the work of Jesus Christ; penance by asserting that Christ's death does not cleanse from *all* of sin, including the temporal punishments; confession, because they denied the existence of a sacramental priesthood in the

New Testament Church, and satisfaction, because they did not believe that anything man could do could even begin to "satisfy" divine justice. Hence, in the sacrament of penance some of the most basic differences between Romanism and the Biblical view espoused by the Reformers can be seen.

It is common for Christians who are involved in evangelizing Roman Catholics to say, "Rome teaches a works-salvation system." It is important that this kind of allegation be understood correctly, both by those who use the phrase and by Roman Catholics. First, Catholics assert that they do not believe that they are saved by their works alone or primarily—Roman Catholic dogmatic statements are legion that deny just this thing. But, most Christians are not asserting that Catholics give no place at all to Christ. It is obvious that the Catholic doctrine speaks of the work of Christ, and asserts that *without* the atonement of Christ, salvation would be impossible.

Having said that, it is important that the Roman Catholic understand what the Christian is trying to say as well (indeed, it is important for the Christian to make sure they have thought through exactly what they mean when they speak of "works-salvation" and, just as importantly, are consistent in their *own* beliefs about the subject). "Works-salvation" would refer to the concept that *man's works are necessary for salvation; that is, that the work of Christ, in and of itself, without human works, actually saves no one at all.* If it is asserted that Christ's work is dependent upon the actions of man, and that God has simply *made a way of salvation available* that is still dependent upon the works of man (whether these works be penances, baptism, whatever), this is "works salvation." Works are a necessary part of this kind of doctrine, and it is this that is said to be in contradiction to the Word of God. It is not necessary that God's grace or mercy not even have a part in salvation for a teaching to be branded "works-salvation." The key issue is whether those works are *necessary and determinative*. Given what we have already seen, Roman Catholicism is *rightly* called a "works-salvation" system.

The final sacrament that deals directly with salvation is that of the Eucharist. As this is the central pillar of the Roman teaching on the atonement and the forgiveness of sin, we now turn to a full discussion of this doctrine.

Chapter 3
The Roman Doctrine of the Sacrifice of the Mass

"With great joy and holy reverence, we approach the great mystery of our Faith: the Sacrament of the Altar, the Eucharist... All the sacraments are oriented towards the Eucharist, the sacrament of sacraments. For our practical Christian living, too, the Eucharist is a focal point. A yardstick used to measure whether there is a living Christianity living in a parish is the percentage of people who receive Communion and regularly participate in Sunday Mass. The more intimate the Christian's relation is to our Eucharistic Savior, the greater and more genuine his living faith will be."[1]

"A Christian who freely neglects for a long time the reception of the Blessed Eucharist, is morally unable to preserve himself in the state of grace for any long time."[2]

"A fully Christian life is unthinkable without participation in the celebration of the Eucharist."[3]

"If there is one mystery of faith around which revolves the whole Catholic liturgy, it is the Eucharist."[4]

"When the priest announces the tremendous words of consecration, he reaches up into the heavens, brings Christ down from His throne, and places Him upon our altar to be offered up again as the Victim for the sins of man. It is a power greater than that of monarchs and emperors: it is greater than that of saints and angels, greater than that of Seraphim and Cherubim.

"Indeed it is greater even than the power of the Virgin Mary. While the Blessed Virgin was the human agency by which Christ became incarnate a single time, the priest brings Christ down from heaven, and renders Him present on our altar as the eternal Victim for the sins of man—not once but a thousand times! The priest speaks and lo! Christ, the eternal and omnipotent God, bows his head in humble obedience to the priest's command.

"Of what sublime dignity is the office of the Christian priest who is thus privileged to act as the ambassador and the vicegerent of Christ on earth! He continues the essential ministry of Christ: he teaches the faithful with the authority of Christ,

> he pardons the penitent sinner with the power of Christ, he offers up again the same sacrifice of adoration and atonement which Christ offered on Calvary. No wonder that the name which spiritual writers are especially fond of applying to the priest is that of *"alter Christus."* For the priest is and should be *another Christ.*[5]

A tremendous amount of literature exists concerning the Roman Catholic doctrine of the Mass. It is known by many names. It can be referred to as "the Eucharistic Sacrifice", the "Sacrifice of the Mass", the "Sacrament of the Mass," etc. There are many facets to the doctrine, and if Catholics like to say that Protestants don't understand the Mass, they need to realize that many of their own people have little understanding of it, either. This author has heard many a differing view of the Mass from practicing Roman Catholics.

Since it is the Mass that primarily demonstrates the Roman view of the work of Christ in atonement, and most strikingly illustrates the error of Roman Catholicism with reference to the Gospel, it is **vital** that the reader have a **full and complete understanding** of the Roman teachings. At the same time, it is recognized that few subjects more often result in charges of "misrepresentation" from Catholic apologists than this one. Any brief, surface discussion of the Mass is bound to cause the Catholic to simply say, "you don't understand what we believe" and dismiss the subject at that point. Hence, it is our intention to cite *extensively* from the *official documents* of the Roman Catholic Church in an honest effort to *accurately* and *fairly* present their belief. Much of the teaching from the Council of Trent will be examined. But, as many in the modern expressions of Romanism look with some disdain upon Trent, the documents of Vatican II will also be examined so that no charge of unbalance can be sustained. Citations from various authors and catechisms will also be provided, sometimes saying things already mentioned, but with slight variation, simply to make sure that the reader (whether Protestant or Catholic) is fully aware of the Roman dogma. We do not multiply citations simply for the sake of show, nor is it my wish to make this chapter somewhat like Leviticus for those who try to read the Bible through in a year. Rather, it is our hope that those who would use this book as a resource would find the many citations valuable for their own research and documentation; whether that reader be a Christian who is seeking to understand the Roman faith so as to share the powerful message of Christ's completed work with Catholics, or a Catholic who is honest enough to deal with the challenges here presented. *It is vital that this section be read and understood, as the arguments from Scripture will take for granted the fact that this material has been mastered.* We will start by providing the decrees and canons from Trent, and will follow this with citations from Vatican II and post-conciliar documents, demonstrating that as far as the theology of the Mass itself, Vatican II changed **nothing**. These citations will show how many questions there are that must be addressed, how many facets of this doctrine to be understood. Some of the questions that the reader should keep in mind while reading these official Catholic pronouncements include:

1) *How important is the doctrine of transubstantiation* (a ten-dollar Latin term meaning "a change of substance": it refers to the idea that the nature of the bread and wine is *changed* into the body and blood of Christ at consecration) *to the doctrine of the Mass*?

2) *What is the relationship between the sacrifice of the Mass and the sacrifice of Christ on the Cross? What are the similarities, according to Rome, and what are the differences?*

3) *How is the Eucharistic sacrifice called "propitiatory"? In what way? What sins does it remit, and for what penalties is it satisfactory?*

These are just some of the questions to keep in mind. Don't get confused about how closely connected many of these concepts are at first: after presenting the dogmatic statements of the Church, we will try to put it all in some kind of order, and make it understandable for the non-Catholic.

Before we dive into Trent, let us re-iterate something that we feel is of utmost importance. *In our culture today, where taking a stand for truth is not popular, (even amongst "Christians" of many of the liberal denominations), there is a great need for integrity in our presentation of the beliefs of those with whom we take issue. If a Christian is to seek to share the Gospel with Catholics, and in so doing identify the Roman church as a non-Christian system, then he absolutely must make sure that his statements are truly reflective of Catholic belief. Any "grand-standing" that results in a caricature, a mis-representation, even if it is not central to the argument, can result in a loss of integrity.* Few non-Catholics are familiar with Trent or Vatican II, but, to be effective in sharing the Gospel with Catholics, even with those Catholics that don't know any more about Trent than the average non-Catholic, a solid understanding of the Roman position is a must. If any Roman Catholic apologists are thinking of saying that this book misrepresents the Catholic faith, they will have to demonstrate it from the same documents that will be cited.

So we begin with the Council of Trent, not because the doctrine of the Mass did not exist prior to Trent, but because Trent had to define the doctrine in opposition to the teachers of the Reformation. It is a simple fact that we tend to be clearer in our definitions when we have a position against which we are responding, and this is the case here as well. The Council of Trent had to defend the Roman position against the likes of Luther and Calvin, and to do so required clear and forceful definitions.

The thirteenth session of the Council of Trent met on October 11th, 1551. The decree promulgated at that time was entitled "Decree Concerning the Most Holy Sacrament of the Eucharist." It consists of eight chapters and 11 canons. This is not the only reference to the Mass by Trent; eleven years later, in 1562, during the twenty-second session, another decree, consisting of nine chapters and nine canons, was presented, entitled "Doctrine Concerning the Sacrifice of the Mass." The reader might note that the two different decrees produced at different times is related to the fact that the Mass is seen in two ways in Catholicism: as a sacrament, and as a sacrifice. The distinction between the two views will be more clearly understood as we move on.

Trent began,

> "The holy, ecumenical and general Council of Trent...for the purpose of setting forth the true and ancient doctrine concerning faith and the sacraments, and of applying a remedy to all the heresies and the other most grievous troubles by which the Church of God is now miserably disturbed and rent into many and

> various parts, yet, even from the outset, has especially desired that it might pull up by the roots the cockles of execrable errors and schisms which the enemy has in these our troubled times disseminated regarding the doctrine, use and worship of the Sacred Eucharist, which our Savior left in His Church as a symbol of that unity and charity with which He wished all Christians to be mutually bonded and united. Wherefore, this holy council, stating that sound and genuine doctrine of the venerable and divine sacrament of the Eucharist, which the Catholic Church, instructed by our Lord Jesus Christ Himself and by His Apostles, and taught by the Holy Ghost who always brings to her mind all truth, had held and will preserve even to the end of the world, forbids all the faithful of Christ to presume henceforth to believe, teach or preach with regard to the most Holy Eucharist otherwise than is explained and defined in this present decree."[6]

Note that the Council admits that the background of their work is that of the Reformation. They insist that the teaching they are about to put forth has *always* been the teaching of Christ's Church (a very arguable claim), and that the Roman Church will *always* believe this, even "to the end of the world." Hence, in reality, these teachings are "irreformable" since to change them would be to admit error in the past—something Romanism simply cannot do when it comes to central issues such as the Mass.

The first thing that the Council affirms is known

as the "Real Presence." What does this mean?

> "First of all, the holy council teaches and openly and plainly confesses that after the consecration of bread and wine, our Lord Jesus Christ, true God and true man, is truly, really and substantially contained in the august sacrament of the Holy Eucharist under the appearance of those sensible things."[7]

The first affirmation is that, following the special words of the consecration by the priest, Jesus Christ is *really* and *substantially* present in the bread and the wine. There can be no "symbolic" understanding of the presence of Christ according to Trent. The actual body of Christ is present during the Mass. Trent cites the passages where Christ says "This is my body" as evidence of their teaching, and says of Christ,

> "...He testified in clear and definite words that He gives them His own body and his own blood. Since these words, recorded by the holy Evangelists and afterwards repeated by St. Paul, embody that proper and clearest meaning in which they were understood by the Fathers, it is a most contemptible action on the part of some contentious and wicked men to twist them into fictitious and imaginary tropes by which the truth of the flesh and blood of Christ is denied, contrary to the universal sense of the Church, which, as the pillar and ground of truth, recognizing with a mind ever grateful and unforgetting this most excellent favor of Christ, has de-

> tested as satanical these untruths devised by impious men."[8]

The next chapter explains some of the reasons *why*, according to Romanism, Christ instituted the sacrament. "...He wished that this sacrament should be received as the spiritual food of souls"[9] and that it should function as "...an antidote whereby we may be freed from daily faults and be preserved from mortal sins." This sacrament, primarily because of the Real Presence, is more "excellent" than any other sacrament. The Council teaches,

> "The most Holy Eucharist has indeed this in common with the other sacraments, that it is a symbol of a sacred thing and a visible form of an invisible grace; but there is found in it this excellent and peculiar characteristic, that the other sacraments then first have the power of sanctifying when one uses them, while in the Eucharist there is the Author Himself of sanctity before it is used. For the Apostles had not yet received the Eucharist from the hands of the Lord, when He Himself told them that what He was giving them is His own body. This has always been the belief of the Church of God, that immediately after the consecration the true body and the true blood of our Lord, together with His soul and divinity exist under the form of bread and wine, the body under the form of bread and the blood under the form of wine *ex vi verborum*;[10] but the same body also under the form of wine and the same blood under

> the form of bread and the soul under both, in virtue of that natural connection and concomitance whereby the parts of Christ the Lord, who hath now risen from the dead, to die no more, are mutually united; also the divinity on account of its admirable hypostatic union with His body and soul."[11]

Note that the *whole* Christ is said to exist under the species of bread and wine; this is how the Roman Church, over a millennia after the death of Christ, could begin to deny the cup to the laity (to the people), for they taught that all of Christ is present under both species, whether bread or wine. Hence, if you take only the bread, you are still getting all of Christ regardless of the fact that you cannot partake of the cup. There was great pressure upon the Council to drop the prohibition of the cup for the laity, but they did not bow to this pressure.

But why is there such an emphasis upon the presence of Christ in the bread and the wine? And how can this be? The next chapter of the decree, Chapter IV, explains:

> "But since Christ our Redeemer declared that to be truly His own body which He offered under the form of bread, it has, therefore, always been a firm belief in the Church of God, and this holy council now declares it anew, that by the consecration of the bread and wine a change is brought about of the whole substance of the bread into the substance of the body of Christ our Lord, and of the whole substance of the wine into the substance of His blood. This change the holy Catholic Church

> properly and appropriately calls transubstantiation."[12]

The body of Christ, then, does not simply *co-exist* with the bread and the wine, but the very *substance* of the bread and wine, after the consecration by the priest, is **gone** and is replaced, instead, with the *very substance of the body of Christ*. Trent did not bother to go into the elaborate schemes worked out by the "Schoolmen" of the preceding centuries as to just how this could happen. To help those who might be somewhat confused, the RCC also teaches that the *accidents*, that is, the appearance of the bread and the wine, stay the same: only, mystery of mysteries, the *accidents* have no natural substance in which to "inhere." The wafer (host) and the wine *look like* bread and wine, but are *really* the body and blood of Christ. There is no question, of course, that if God wanted to do such a thing, He could. The question is whether He teaches in His Word that He does so. We shall see that He does not.[13]

Many of the peculiar doctrines revolving around the Mass come from this notion of *transubstantiation*. The concept of the "Eucharistic Sacrifice," for example, can be seen to be intimately related to what we have here in the presence of the body of Christ on the altar in the form of bread and wine. So, too, is the worship and veneration of the host, for if it is the body of Christ, then God is physically present in the Mass. Trent continued,

> "There is, therefore, no room for doubt that all the faithful of Christ may, in accordance with a custom always received in the Catholic Church, give to this most holy sacrament in veneration the worship of *latria*,[14] which is due to the true God...The holy council declares, more-

> over, that the custom that this sublime and venerable sacrament be celebrated with special veneration and solemnity every year on a fixed festival day, and that it be borne reverently and with honor in processions through the streets and public places, was very piously and religiously introduced into the Church of God."[15]

The next chapter deals with the "reserving of the Holy Eucharist in a sacred place..." This would refer to a monstrance, pyx, ciborium, or tabernacle, where unused but consecrated hosts are kept. The RCC believes that once a host is consecrated, and hence *transubstantiated* into the body of Christ, it remains that way. Therefore, by placing a consecrated host into the tabernacle in a church, Christ is physically present.[16] This should explain for the non-Catholic why Catholics "genuflect" or bow on one knee, the action frequently being accompanied by crossing oneself. The Catholic is acknowledging the presence of Christ Himself in the tabernacle or monstrance.

The final two chapters of the decree deal with the need of confession of all mortal sins before partaking of the Eucharist, and the uses of the Sacrament itself. These chapters are then followed by a list of canons, eleven in number, which pronounce the "anathema" on various false teachings about the sacrament of the Eucharist. Below are some of those that are relevant to the current discussion:

> "Canon 1. If anyone denies that in the sacrament of the most Holy Eucharist are contained truly, really and substantially the body and blood together with the soul and divinity of our Lord Jesus Christ, and

> consequently the whole Christ, but says that He is in it only as in a sign, or figure or force, let him be anathema.
>
> "Canon 2. If anyone says that in the sacred and holy sacrament of the Eucharist the substance of the bread and wine remains conjointly with the body and blood of our Lord Jesus Christ, and denies that wonderful and singular change of the whole substance of the bread into the body and the whole substance of the wine into the blood, the appearances only of bread and wine remaining, which change the Catholic Church most aptly calls transubstantiation, let him be anathema.
>
> "Canon 6. If anyone says that in the holy sacrifice of the Eucharist, Christ, the only begotten Son of God, is not to be adored with the worship of *latria*, also outwardly manifested, and is consequently neither to be venerated with a special festive solemnity, not to be solemnly borne about in procession according to the laudable and universal rite and custom of holy Church, or is not to be set publicly before the people to be adored and that the adorers thereof are idolaters, let him be anathema.
>
> "Canon 8. If anyone says that Christ received in the Eucharist is received spiritually only and not also sacramentally and really, let him be anathema."[17]

So far, then, we have the Roman Catholic doctrine of transubstantiation presented in the sacrament of the Eucharist. It has been clearly set forth that the body and blood of Christ is really and substantially present following the consecration. But, we might well ask, what is the significance of this? The twenty-second session took up the subject under the title, "Doctrine Concerning the Sacrifice of the Mass." The first two chapters of this decree are so important to the argument of this work that we have chosen to reproduce most of their text below:

> "Since under the former Testament, according to the testimony of the Apostle Paul, there was no perfection because of the weakness of the Levitical priesthood, there was need, God the Father of mercies so ordaining, that another priest should arise according to the order of Melchisedech, our Lord Jesus Christ, who might perfect and lead to perfection as many as were to be sanctified. He, therefore, our God and Lord, though He was by His death about to offer Himself once upon the altar of the cross to God the Father that He might there accomplish an eternal redemption, nevertheless, that His priesthood might not come to an end with His death, at the last supper, on the night He was betrayed, that He might leave to His beloved spouse the Church a visible sacrifice, such as the nature of man requires, whereby that bloody sacrifice once to be accomplished on the cross might be represented, the memory thereof remain even to the end of the world, and its salutary effects applied to the remission of those sins which we daily commit, declaring Himself constituted a priest

> forever according to the order of Melchisedech, offered up to God the Father His own body and blood under the form of bread and wine, and under the forms of those same things gave to the Apostles, whom He then made priests of the New Testament, that they might partake, commanding them and their successors in the priesthood by these words to do likewise: *Do this in commemoration of me*, as the Catholic Church has always understood and taught. For having celebrated the ancient Passover which the multitude of the children of Israel sacrificed in memory of their departure from Egypt, He instituted a new Passover, namely, Himself, to be immolated[18] under visible signs by the Church through the priests in memory of His own passage from this world to the Father, when by shedding of His blood He redeemed and delivered us from the power of darkness and translated us into his kingdom."[19]

Chapter 2 continues,

> "And inasmuch as in this divine sacrifice which is celebrated in the mass is contained and immolated in an unbloody manner the same Christ who once offered Himself in a blood manner on the altar of the cross, the holy council teaches that this is truly propitiatory and has this effect, that if we, contrite and penitent, with sincere heart and upright faith, with fear and reverence, draw nigh to God, we

> obtain mercy and find grace in seasonable aid. For, appeased by this sacrifice, the Lord grants the grace and gift of penitence and pardons even the gravest crimes and sins. For the victim is one and the same, the same now offering by the ministry of priests who then offered Himself on the cross, the manner alone of offering being different. The fruits of that bloody sacrifice, it is well understood, are received most abundantly through this unbloody one, so far is the latter from derogating in any way from the former. Wherefore, according to the tradition of the Apostles, it is rightly offered not only for the sins, punishments, satisfactions and other necessities of the faithful who are living, but also for those departed in Christ but not yet fully purified."[20]

That is a lot of material to digest. A few comments on these chapters should help in organizing their content.

First, it is claimed that Christ, in instituting the Eucharist at the Lord's Supper, did so for a number of reasons: first, to leave to His Church "a visible sacrifice" which, the council says, "the nature of man requires." The Mass, then, is to cause the memory of the bloody sacrifice of the cross to remain to the end of the world. But, *very importantly*, the Mass is also to "apply" the effects of the cross "to the remission of those sins which we daily commit," i.e., the remission of venial sins.

Next, we see that the Roman Church claims that in the Last Supper the Lord Jesus *actually offered Himself as a sacrifice in the bread and the wine*. This takes place **before** the sacrifice of the cross. When Jesus took the bread and said, "this is My body..." the RCC teaches that

He had actually changed the bread into His own body,[21] and in so doing offered the first "Sacrifice of the Mass." Since He then told the disciples to do the same thing, then it follows (according to this line of reasoning) that He did at this time ordain the Apostles as "priests of the New Testament, that they might partake, commanding them and their successors in the priesthood by these words to do likewise." This new institution, then, is to be repeated by priests down through the centuries "in memory of His own passage from this world to the Father...."

Chapter 2 asserts that the sacrifice of the Mass, then, since it is the same Christ who is present who died on Calvary, (note the importance, then, of transubstantiation) then the *unbloody* sacrifice of the Mass is "truly propitiatory..." God is said to be "appeased" by this sacrifice, which differs from the sacrifice of the cross only in the *manner* of the offering, the cross being bloody, the Mass unbloody. The effect of the sacrifice, then, is that "the Lord grants the grace and gift of penitence and pardons even the gravest crimes and sins." Here we are told that the sacrifice of the Mass *is able to bring about forgiveness of sins*. In fact, the "fruits" of the bloody sacrifice of Christ on the cross, it is asserted, "are received most abundantly through this unbloody one...."

The sacrifice of the Mass is offered "for the sins, punishments, satisfactions and other necessities of the faithful who are living" as well as for those who "departed in Christ" but who were not yet "fully purified."[22] Therefore, we are told that Masses are effective for those living *and* the dead, though in different ways. The sacrifice is effective for the living, though in a very limited sense, for the effect of the propitiation of sin is limited only to those sins committed in the past, not future, *and*, though not expressly said in so many words, the "measurement of the punishments of sins remitted is proportional, in the case of the living, to the degree of perfection of their disposition."[23] That is, the *degree* of forgiveness is dependent upon the *intention* and *disposition* of the person to whom the benefits of the Mass are applied; if a person is not perfectly contrite in heart, then the effect of the Mass is less than it might be otherwise. What one basically has is a teaching that says that the sacrifice of the Mass, though supposedly a "renewal" or "representation" of the sacrifice of the Cross, is *limited* in its effect by the disposition of human beings.[24]

As with the previous chapter, this one is followed by a list of canons, most of which are relevant to our inquiry:

> "Canon 1. If anyone says that in the mass a true and real sacrifice is not offered to God; or that to be offered is nothing else than that Christ is given to us to eat, let him be anathema.
>
> "Canon 2. If anyone says that by those words, *Do this for a commemoration of me*, Christ did not institute the Apostles priests; or did not ordain that they and other priests should offer His own body and blood, let him be anathema.
>
> "Canon 3. If anyone says that the sacrifice of the mass is one only of praise and thanksgiving; or that it is a mere commemoration of the sacrifice consummated on the cross but not a propitiatory one; or that it profits him only who receives, and ought not to be offered for the living and the dead, for sins, punishments, satisfactions, and other necessities, let him be

> anathema.
> "Canon 4. If anyone says that by the sacrifice of the mass a blasphemy is cast upon the most holy sacrifice of Christ consummated on the cross; or that the former derogates from the latter, let him be anathema.[25]
> "Canon 5. If anyone says that it is a deception to celebrate masses in honor of the saints and in order to obtain their intercession with God, as the Church intends, let him be anathema.
> "Canon 6. If anyone says that the canon of the mass contains errors and is therefore to be abrogated, let him be anathema."[26]

Following these statements is a section on things to be observed and avoided in the celebration of Mass. One section is important to note as we close out our investigation of Trent's teachings on the Mass:

> "And since we must confess that no other work can be performed by the faithful that is so holy and divine as this awe-inspiring mystery; wherein that life-giving victim by which we are reconciled to the Father is daily immolated on the altar by priests, it is also sufficiently clear that all effort and attention must be directed to the end that it be performed with the greatest possible interior cleanness and purity of heart and exterior evidence of devotion and piety."[27]

These then are the teachings of Trent on the Mass.

What can be concluded from these quotations? Surely the whole of the Roman doctrine is here in basic outline form. Roman dogmatic theologies attempt to answer the myriad of questions that are raised by these teachings, and some of their conclusions will be reviewed below. But for our purposes let us summarize Trent's teachings, so that we can compare them with the statements we will find in the teaching of Vatican II:

1) *Jesus Christ is truly, really and substantially present in the sacrament of the Eucharist following the words of consecration.*

2) *Transubstantiation involves the change of the whole substance of the bread into the substance of the body of Christ, and the change of the whole substance of the wine into the blood of Christ.*

3) *Since Christ is said to be really present in the Eucharist, the elements themselves, following consecration, are worthy of worship.*

4) *The Sacrifice of the Mass is properly called "propitiatory" in that it brings about pardon of sin.*

5) *In the institution of the Mass at the Lord's Supper, Christ offered His own body and blood to the Father in the signs of the bread and wine, and in so doing ordained the Apostles as priests of the New Testament.*

6) *The Sacrifice of the Mass is properly offered for sins, punishments, satisfactions and other necessities, not only for the living, but for the dead as well.*

7) *Finally, anyone who denies the truthfulness of any of these proclamations is under the anathema of God.*

So spoke Trent, and so the Roman Catholic Church has taught ever since. The four hundred years between Trent and Vatican II (which opened on October 11, 1962) was shaped and formed by Trent's decrees. But what of today? Have we been reviewing a ghost, a mere apparition, something that is not believed today? Are those many Roman Catholics right who have said to us, "oh, Vatican II changed all that"? Did Vatican II rid the Roman system of these teachings, presented so clearly, and forcefully (one does not anathematize people for trivial reasons), four hundred years earlier? Or are these statements of Trent still valid today? What *did* Vatican II have to say? To this we shall now turn.

Vatican II and the Mass

The first completed work of the Vatican II council was the "Constitution on the Sacred Liturgy." It was promulgated on December 4, 1963. The Mass is of central significance to this document, as the following quotations will demonstrate.

What did this most modern of Roman councils say about the Mass? In section 2 we read,

> "For it is through the liturgy, especially the divine Eucharistic Sacrifice, that 'the work of our redemption is exercised.'"[28]

In speaking of the role of Christ in Roman liturgy, the Council, far from disapproving of Trent's formulations, even quoted from them:

> "To accomplish so great a work, Christ is always present in His Church, especially in her liturgical celebrations. He is present in the sacrifice of the Mass, not

> only in the person of His minister, 'the same one now offering, through the ministry of priests, who formerly offered himself on the cross,' but especially under the Eucharistic species."[29]

Does Vatican II see the Eucharist sacramentally? Most definitely:

> "The renewal in the Eucharist of the covenant between the Lord and man draws the faithful into the compelling love of Christ and sets them afire. From the liturgy, therefore, and especially from the Eucharist, as from a fountain, grace is channeled to us...."[30]

Chapter 2 of the decree on liturgy is specifically entitled, *"The Most Sacred Mystery of the Eucharist."* It begins with section 47:

> "At the Last Supper, on the night when He was betrayed, our Savior instituted the Eucharistic Sacrifice of His Body and Blood. He did this in order to perpetuate the sacrifice of the Cross throughout the centuries until He should come again, and so to entrust to His beloved spouse, the Church, a memorial of His death and resurrection: a sacrament of love, a sign of unity, a bond of charity, a paschal banquet in which Christ is consumed, the mind is filled with grace, and a pledge of future glory is given to us."[31]

Vatican II speaks with language heavily influenced, it is

obvious, by Trent:

> "They should be instructed by God's word and be refreshed at the table of the Lord's body; they should give thanks to God; by offering the Immaculate Victim, not only through the hands of the priest, but also with him, they should learn to offer themselves too."[32]

A small variance from Trent is found in the fact that if the bishop thinks it proper, communion under both kinds may be granted. Of course, this is not a change in the theology at all, and in fact, in stating this, the Vatican II Council *reaffirmed* the validity of the dogmatic stance of Trent:

> "The dogmatic principles which were laid down by the Council of Trent remaining intact, communion under both kinds may be granted when the bishops think fit...."[33]

One will search in vain through the documents of Vatican II for anything that would even begin to suggest that the doctrinal position of Trent on the Mass has been in any way abrogated or changed. Indeed, the Council did not need to dwell on the theological aspects of the Mass at all, for Trent's definitions were taken as normative. This view of the Mass can be seen in other decrees of the Council. In the decree on Ecumenism we read,

> "The ecclesial Communities separated from us lack that fullness of unity with us which should flow from baptism, and we believe that especially because of the lack

> of the sacrament of orders they have not preserved the genuine and total reality of the Eucharistic mystery."[34]

And in the *"Dogmatic Constitution on the Church"* the continued belief in the Eucharistic sacrifice, as defined by Trent, is seen:

> "As often as the sacrifice of the cross in which "Christ, our passover, has been sacrificed"...is celebrated on an altar, the work of our redemption is carried on. At the same time, in the sacrament of the Eucharistic bread the unity of all believers who form one body in Christ...is both expressed and brought about."[35]

> "Taking part in the Eucharistic Sacrifice, which is the fount and apex of the whole Christian life, they offer the divine Victim to God, and offer themselves along with It."[36]

> "They exercise this sacred function of Christ most of all in the Eucharistic liturgy or synaxis. There, acting in the person of Christ, and proclaiming His mystery, they join in the offering of the faithful to the sacrifice of their Head. Until the coming of the Lord... they represent and apply in the Sacrifice of the Mass the one sacrifice of the New Testament, namely the sacrifice of Christ offering Himself once and for all to His Father as a spotless victim."[37]

All of these statements are perfectly in line with the theological standards already examined from the Council of Trent. Nothing has changed. Indeed, the *post-conciliar* documents bring this out with great clarity. In a document issued on May 25, 1967 entitled "*Eucharisticum Mysterium,*" we read in reference to the worship due the sacrament,

> "For even in the reserved sacrament he is to be adored because he is substantially present there through that conversion of bread and wine which, as the Council of Trent tells us, is most aptly named transubstantiation."[38]

In another document released May 29, 1969, entitled "*Memoriale Domini,*" we find these words:

> "The fact that the lay person is now able to receive holy communion in the hand should not suggest to him that this is ordinary bread, or just any sacred object. Rather ought it to strengthen his sense of his dignity as a member of the Mystical Body of Christ, of which baptism and the grace of the Eucharist make him a part. He will thus experience an increase of faith in the great reality of the Body and Blood of the Lord which he touches with his hands. His respectful attitude should be proportionate to what he is doing."[39]

But the most in-depth discussion is found in the "*General Instruction on the Roman Missal.*" Here the definitions of Trent are not only reaffirmed, but are expanded upon:

"The sacrificial character of the Mass was solemnly defined by the Council of Trent in accordance with the universal tradition of the Church. The Second Vatican Council has enunciated this same teaching once again, and made this highly significant comment: 'At the Last Supper our Saviour instituted the eucharistic sacrifice of his Body and Blood. He did this in order to perpetuate the sacrifice of the Cross until he should come again; and he wished to entrust to his beloved spouse, the Church, a memorial of his death and resurrection.' The Council's teaching on this point finds an enduring expression in the texts of the Mass. A sentence from the Leonine sacramentary: 'Whenever the memorial of this sacrifice is celebrated, the work of our redemption is accomplished' expresses succinctly the very doctrine set forth anew in suitable and accurate terms in the Eucharistic prayers. In these the priest, during the anamnesis (prayer of remembrance), addresses himself to God in the name of all the people; he gives thanks to God and offers to him a holy and living sacrifice, the Church's offering, the Victim whose death has reconciled man with God; he prays that the Body and Blood of Christ may be the acceptable sacrifice which brings salvation to the whole world...From this we learn that the sacrifice of the Cross and its sacramental renewal in the Mass are, apart from the difference in the manner of

> offering, one and the same sacrifice; it is this sacramental renewal which Christ the Lord instituted at the Last Supper and commanded his apostles to celebrate in his memory. The Mass is therefore a sacrifice of praise, of thanksgiving, or propitiation and of satisfaction.
>
> "In the celebration of the Mass there is proclaimed the wonderful mystery of the real presence of Christ our Lord under the eucharistic species. The Second Vatican Council and other magisterial pronouncements of the Church have confirmed this truth in the same sense and the same words as those in which the Council of Trent defined it as an article of faith."[40]

Hence it is indisputable that the teachings of Trent on the Mass—including the articles on transubstantiation, the sacrificial nature of the Eucharist, and its propitiatory nature—remain valid expressions of Roman Catholic teaching, fully representative of the teaching of the Pope and his bishops to this day.

It would probably be sufficient simply to cite these dogmatic works of the RCC and leave it at that. But the question could profitably be asked, what of popular belief? Do the catechisms and doctrinal works of Catholic theologians reflect a real belief in such things as transubstantiation? Do Catholic writers really feel that this ceremony is a sacrifice, capable of pardoning sin and remitting penalties?

James Cardinal Gibbons wrote in defense of the RCC in 1876. In speaking of the Mass, he said,

> "The sacrifice of the Mass is the consecration of the bread and wine into the

> body and blood of Christ, and the oblation of this body and blood to God, by the ministry of the Priest, for a perpetual memorial of Christ's sacrifice on the cross. The Sacrifice of the Mass is identical with that of the cross, both having the same victim and High Priest—Jesus Christ.
>
> "The only difference consists in the manner of the oblation. Christ was offered up on the cross in a bloody manner, and in the Mass He is offered up in an unbloody manner. On the cross He purchased our ransom, and in the Eucharistic Sacrifice the price of that ransom is applied to our souls. Hence, all the efficacy of the Mass is derived from the sacrifice of Calvary."[41]

These sentiments are perfectly in line with the teachings of Trent, even to the point of utilizing the same categories and words. The main elements are repeated: the physical presence of Christ, the sacrificial nature of the sacrament, the difference of bloody versus unbloody, the idea that in the Mass the "price of that ransom is applied" to souls. This American Archbishop of Baltimore surely accepted, and *taught as God's truth*, the view of the Mass already seen.

Dr. Ludwig Ott, a well-known Roman Catholic theologian, wrote the **Fundamentals of Catholic Dogma** prior to the Vatican II Council. He cites heavily from the decrees of Trent in his definitions and formulations. In opening the discussion on transubstantiation he writes,

> "Christ becomes present in the Sacrament of the Altar by the transformation of the whole substance of the bread into His

> Body and of the whole substance of the wine into His Blood."[42]

Later he affirms that "The Holy Mass is a true and proper Sacrifice"[43] and "In the sacrifice of the Mass, Christ's Sacrifice on the Cross is made present, its memory is celebrated, and its saving power is applied."[44] He goes on to explain,

> "While the Sacrifice on the Cross is an absolute sacrifice, as it is neither the commemoration of a past sacrifice nor the archetype of a future sacrifice, the Sacrifice of the Mass is a relative sacrifice, as it is essentially linked to the Sacrifice on the Cross. [Ott then cites from Trent and then continues]...The sacrifice of the Mass is the presenting again of the Sacrifice of the Cross, in so far as the sacrificial Body and the sacrificial Blood of Christ are made present under separate species, thus symbolically representing the real separation of the body and blood of Christ on the Cross...But it is not a mere commemorative celebration...it is also a true and proper sacrifice. Finally, the sacrifice of the Mass is the means whereby the fruits of the Sacrifice of the Cross are applied to mankind in need of salvation."[45]

Ott's perspectives *before* Vatican II are shared by *many* writers *after it.* So that the reader will not have to read the same things over and over again, let it simply be noted that the major aspects of the doctrine of the Mass are presented by:

Matthias Premm in his **Dogmatic Theology for the Laity**, in sections found on pages 346 through 368;

Anthony Wilhelm in **Christ Among Us**, in sections found on pages 215 through 255;

John Hardon in **The Catholic Catechism**, in sections found on pages 457 through 481;[46]

Peter Stravinskas in **The Catholic Response**, pages 83 through 93;[47]

William Ogrodowski in his **A Catholic Book of the Mass**, pages 67 through 75;[48]

and Alan Schreck, in his **Catholic and Christian**, pages 132 through 140.[49]

Why are we so adamant in insisting that the Catholic Church teaches that the Mass is a truly propitiatory sacrifice? Why list authors (and the list could be extended almost indefinitely) who say the same things? The reason is this: *many* both within and outside of Roman Catholicism do not understand the major aspects of the doctrine of the Mass. It is our belief that the teachings introduced into evidence thus far are directly contradicted by the teaching of the Bible. When the words of Scripture are introduced, and the Bible's teaching presented, the Roman position, if it has been accurately portrayed, will be clearly seen by all to be in utter contradiction to the doctrine of Scripture *and*, since great pains have been taken to make sure that the Roman position is understood, only by dishonesty could anyone dismiss the Biblical truths by saying that the Roman Church does not teach something contrary to the Bible. If a Catholic distrusts our presentation of the

Catholic position to this point, then *please*, put a marker at this page, go get any or all of the above cited works, *and read it for yourself!* We, unlike the magisterium of the RCC, do not claim to have any special authority whereby you are bound to believe everything we say as if it came from God. *Check it out for yourself!* Look up the references, read the end notes, not only when discussing Romanism, but even more so when we move on to dealing with the Bible's teaching. *Don't believe anything we have to say just because we say it—and don't believe what you are told by someone claiming "authority" until you have checked out their credentials in the light of God's revelation in the Bible.* Anyone who comes along and says, "believe what I have to say simply because **I say it!**" is not presenting a Christian position. Even the Lord Jesus, who surely had the authority to speak and be believed simply on the basis of the majesty of His Person, referred to God's Holy Word as authoritative and final on more than one occasion.

The Mass in Brief

In an attempt to bring the central issues into focus, and provide a solid basis for the Biblical discussion of the work of Christ that will be presented below, a definition and presentation of the Roman doctrine of the Mass is here provided that purposefully emphasizes those teachings that are central to this discussion:

The Roman Catholic Church's teaching on the Eucharist can be divided into three sections: one, the teaching of *transubstantiation*; two, the concept of the Mass as a *propitiatory sacrifice*; and three, the *effects* of participation in the Mass itself.

In regards to the first, the RCC teaches that, after the consecration of the bread and wine, the *substance* of the bread and wine is *changed*, or *transubstantiated*. The *substance* of the bread and wine no longer exists; rather, the *substance* of the body and blood (together with the soul and divinity) of Christ is present. The *appearance* of bread and wine remains, but in *reality* Christ is "present on the altar" after the consecration.

Secondly, since Christ is physically present on the altar, the Mass is properly said to be a *sacrifice*. This sacrifice is effective for sins, punishments, satisfactions, and "other necessities of the faithful who are living," and it is also effective in reducing the punishments undergone by the "poor souls" who are in purgatory. Catholic councils and theologians are careful to maintain that the Eucharist is not a *new* sacrifice, or *another* sacrifice than that of the Cross; rather, it is claimed that the efficacy of the Mass comes from Calvary, and the Mass is the means whereby the fruit of redemption, won on the Cross, is *applied* to the individual. The *mode* of sacrifice is admitted to differ; that is, the Cross is a bloody sacrifice, the Mass an unbloody one.

Thirdly, this sacrifice is said to be *propitiatory* in that it remits sins; yet, this needs to be understood within the Catholic definitions of the terms. Mortal sin is not immediately remitted by the Mass, but instead "grace and the gift of repentance" is granted, resulting in the pardon of "even the gravest crimes and sins." Temporal punishments due to sins where the guilt and *eternal punishment* (to be distinguished from *temporal*) have been remitted can be *satisfied* by the sacrifice of the Mass, but *how much* of one's temporal punishments are remitted by any one participation in a Mass is dependent upon the *disposition* of the person communicating; that is, not *all* of one's temporal punishments are automatically remitted by the Mass. Furthermore, the Mass is satisfactory only up until the present time, just as baptism, in Catholicism, is in reference only to past sins, not to any future sins, and the position one gains by partaking of either of these sacraments can be lost through mortal sin at a later time. The *propitiatory* nature of the Mass is said to be derived from the fact that it is the same Priest (Christ) and the same Victim (Christ) in both the sacrifice of the Cross (which was surely propitiatory) and in the Mass. The *fruits* of Calvary, then, are "channeled" through the Mass, and applied to the individual in this way. The *propitiation* obtained through the Mass is *finite* in its effects, which is why the faithful Catholic can attend literally thousands of Masses and yet still need time in purgatory to "finish" the process of purification and sanctification.

This, then, is the doctrine of the Mass, which, we are told, one cannot disbelieve and expect to be saved. To reject these things is to be placed under the anathema of "mother church," and to be lost forever. At the same time, this is the first of the two ways in which we will demonstrate the *fatal flaw* of Romanism: here a way of *propitiation, of satisfaction for sins*, is presented **which is other than the final and completed work of Christ on Calvary.** But there is another way in which this flaw can be demonstrated. It is to be found in the Catholic doctrine on indulgences and purgatory.

Chapter 4
The Roman Doctrine of Purgatory

> Since the Catholic Church, instructed by the Holy Ghost, has, following the sacred writings and the ancient tradition of the Fathers, taught in sacred councils and very recently in this ecumenical council that there is a purgatory, and that the souls there detained are aided by the suffrages of the faithful and chiefly by the acceptable sacrifice of the altar, the holy council commands the bishops that they strive diligently to the end that the sound doctrine of purgatory, transmitted by the Fathers and sacred councils, be believed and maintained by the faithful of Christ, and be everywhere taught and preached.[1]

So spoke and defined the Council of Trent on the subject of purgatory. No one would say that this subject took a great deal of the Council's attention, and the decree concerning purgatory is not a major aspect of the documents of the Council. But the doctrine of purgatory itself is not to be judged a minor teaching because of Trent's simple re-affirmation of its existence. Purgatory, and the related doctrine of *indulgences*, is closely connected with the beliefs already examined regarding sin, salvation, and the work of Christ, and, as we shall see, figures prominently in the false teachings of Rome with reference to the forgiveness of sins through the death of Christ.

Those who are in purgatory, frequently styled the "poor souls," were described as "those departed in Christ but not yet fully purified" in the second chapter of the decree on the sacrifice of the Mass cited above. Hence, these are individuals who die in a state of grace, yet still have temporal punishments for sins, or venial sins themselves, from which they have not been purged. John Hardon explained it this way:

> "The reason of faith is that nothing defiled can enter heaven, and therefore anyone less than perfect must first be purified before he can be admitted to the vision of God. In more concrete terms, which have been carved out of centuries of the Church's reflection on revelation, there exists purgatory, in which the souls of the just who die with the stains of sins are cleansed by expiation before they are admitted to heaven. They can be helped, however, by the intercession of the faithful on earth.
>
> "Who are the souls of the just? They are those that leave the body in the state of sanctifying grace and are therefore destined by right to enter heavenly glory. Their particular judgment was favorable, although conditional. They must first be cleansed before they can see the face of God. The condition is always fulfilled.

> "When we speak of 'stains of sins,' the expression is consciously ambivalent. It first means the temporal punishment due to venial or mortal sins already forgiven as to guilt but not fully remitted as to penalty when a person dies. It may also mean the venial sins themselves, not forgiven as to guilt or punishment before death."[2]

It can readily be seen how related this teaching is to what has been seen in the Mass: the concept of sin being *partially* forgiven, that is, the *guilt* and *eternal punishment* being remitted in Christ, but the temporal punishment, the "stains of sin" remaining, requiring a further "purging" of the person's soul. An important aspect to grasp is the fact that the Roman Catholic can confess on a regular basis in the sacrament of Confession, he or she can attend Mass just about every time it is possible to do so, and *yet remain impure, imperfect, stained by sin*. A person who has attended a thousand masses will still end up in purgatory, for the Mass, being dependent upon the individual's disposition for its expiatory efficacy,[3] is not capable of *fully and completely* perfecting those to whom it is applied; then again, neither is the sacrament of Confession, for the priest, in remitting the confessed sins, does not normally loose the temporal punishments, but assigns penances, works, etc. to make satisfaction.

We further see that the *sufferings* of these souls in purgatory is seen as being *propitiatory or satisfactory*. This is a very important concept to understand as well. The Catholic doctrine is here presenting the concept that suffering on the part of the sinner has *merit* before God relative to the forgiveness of sin or its punishments. This is in line with Ott, who says,

> "The remission of the venial sins which are not yet remitted, occurs, according to the teaching of St. Thomas (De male, 7,11), as it does in this life, by an act of contrition deriving from charity and performed with the help of grace. This act of contrition, which is presumably awakened immediately after entry into the purifying fire, does not, however, effect the abrogation or the diminution of the punishment for sins, since in the other world there is no longer any possibility of merit.
>
> "The temporal punishments for sins are atoned for in the purifying fire by the so-called suffering of atonement (satis-passio), that is, by the willing bearing of the expiatory punishments imposed by God."[4]

Note in passing, that the purging of these souls of the "stain of sin" is *not* said to be by the work of Christ; it is their *own suffering*, or as Ott put it, by the "suffering of atonement," that the temporal punishments for sin are satisfied. *It is not, then, by the suffering of Christ, but by the suffering of the person, that these sins are removed.*

Furthermore, it is taught that these souls in purgatory can be helped by those who are still alive upon the earth. Gibbons writes,

> "The Catholic Church teaches that, besides a place of eternal torments for the wicked and of everlasting rest for the righteous, there exists in the next life a middle state of temporary punishment, allotted for those who have died in venial

> sin, or who have not satisfied the justice of God for sins already forgiven. She also teaches that, although the souls consigned to this intermediate state, commonly called purgatory, cannot help themselves, they may be aided by suffrages of the faithful on earth."[5]

How can the actions of the "faithful" on earth have any effect upon the souls in purgatory? To understand this, we must take a small detour from our study of purgatory to understand some related concepts: particularly, the *merit of the saints, supererogation, treasury of merit, and indulgences.*

From some of the earliest documents of the post-Apostolic era, it is known that *prayers for the dead* were practiced by Christians. The Roman Catholic Church, and its apologists, almost universally assume that since this is the case, then this must also mean that the doctrine of *purgatory* was believed as well. But this simply does not follow. As William Cathcart wrote,

> "But these prayers never hint that the departed are in a place of purification by suffering. They were offered up for all the Church triumphant, including the Virgin Mary; they were often thanksgivings for their deliverance out of the sorrows of this life; they were appeals to God for his mercy on account of the imperfections with which they left the world; they used these prayers as an expression of their conviction that the departed were in the enjoyment of an endless life; they were presented to God that he might have a special care over the faithful disembod-

ied, and give them a glorious resurrection in the appointed time."[6]

Over time, however, and particularly under the influence of Gregory I, also called "the Great," a stream of concepts came together to form the basis of the modern doctrine of purgatory. The first concept came from the years when martyrs were a part of the Christian Church's experience on a regular basis. People came to look at martyrs as special people, specially graced by God. Eventually, the martyrs were looked at as people who not only entered directly into heaven upon their death, but, since they were *so holy*, they earned *extra merit*, more than was needed for their own salvation. This *extra merit* is also known by the term "*supererogation,*" where a person does more good deeds than are necessary for their own salvation. To this was added the idea that the shedding of just one drop of Christ's blood would have been sufficient for the salvation of the world; but, since all of His blood was shed, there exists a super over-abundance of merit, made up of the extra-merits of Christ, as well as of the saints and the Virgin Mary.[7] All these together make up the "*treasury of merit*" that is available as an "aid" for those seeking salvation. This treasury, however, is under the direct control of the Roman Catholic Church, and the extra merit contained therein is dispensed solely through the RCC.

From this idea of the "spiritual treasure" of the Church came the next concept to be understood: that of the *indulgence*. O'Brien defines an indulgence as "the remission of the *temporal punishment* due to sin after the sin itself has been forgiven."[8] He continues by noting the Roman concept of sin and its twofold penalty (*eternal* and *temporal* punishments), and, after asserting that the *eternal* punishment is remitted by confession, he says that the *temporal* punishment may or may not be remitted. He continues,

> "If it is not forgiven, it may be remitted: (1) through the propitiatory efficacy of deeds of penance and virtue, and (2) through the gaining of indulgences attached by the Church to certain works of charity and piety.
>
> "Basic in this whole conception is the idea that even after the eternal punishment due to mortal sin is remitted, there may still remain temporal punishment... To satisfy the requirement of God's justice for such temporal punishment, and thereby to remit it, is the function of indulgences."[9]

How do indulgences function? What is the relationship between the "treasury of merit" and indulgences? O'Brien says,

> "Since Christ suffered far more than was necessary to redeem us, and since there resulted from His death a fund of infinite satisfaction, it follows that there has been created a vast and inexhaustible treasury which the Church may draw upon in payment of temporal punishment. This spiritual treasury has been increased by the superabundant satisfaction of the Blessed Virgin and of the saints."[10]

Since Rome claims that the "keys of the Church" were given to Peter, and the Pope claims to be the successor of Peter, then the Roman Pontiff has the "keys" to this "treasury" and is able to disperse its riches to individuals as he sees fit. The application of some of the satisfactions of this treasure for the remission of the temporal punishment for sin is an *indulgence*.

Indulgences can only be gained by the living, but they can be applied either to the living or the dead. When applied to the dead, they are said to remit, in part, some portion of the time of purging of the "poor soul." Ott admits that in reference to the souls in purgatory "their operation is uncertain," and O'Brien says,

> "While we piously believe that the individual soul will be benefited to some degree, we cannot say with certainty that it will be applied in its entirety to that particular soul."[11]

Surely this modern position is less strident than the one manifested prior to the Reformation. At that time, as was noted above, the Roman See was utilizing the sale of indulgences for money as a means of revenue for the building of St. Peter's. People were not told that the "operation" of indulgences in reference to the dead is "uncertain," for that would hardly sell! Rather, it is reported that the young boys who would accompany John Tetzel in his indulgence-selling adventures would sing this little ditty:

"When a coin in the coffer
rings,
a soul from purgatory
springs!
When a coin in the coffer
rings,
a soul from purgatory
springs,

A soul from purgatory
springs!"[12]

The promise was based upon the Papal authority, and it was Luther's rejection of Tetzel's indulgence selling that led Eck to question Luther's commitment to the authority of the Papacy, and eventually forced Luther to reject any authority that would sell God's forgiveness and prey upon the weaknesses of the people.

The corruption associated with the selling of indulgences is reflected in the words of the Council of Trent. While continuing the theological teaching, the Council attempted to curb the obvious and gross pillage of the people that was prevalent only a few years before. They taught,

> "Since the power of granting indulgences was conferred by Christ on the Church, and she has even in the earliest times made use of that power divinely given to her, the holy council teaches and commands that the use of indulgences, most salutary to the Christian people and approved by the authority of the holy councils, is to be retained in the Church, and it condemns with anathema those who assert that they are useless or deny that there is in the Church the power of granting them. In granting them, however, it desires that in accordance with the ancient and approved custom in the Church moderation be observed, lest by too great facility ecclesiastical discipline be weakened. But desiring that the abuses which have become connected with them, and by reason of which this excellent

> name of indulgences is blasphemed by the heretics, be amended and corrected, it ordains in a general way by the present decree that all evil traffic in them, which has been a most prolific source of abuses among the Christian people, be absolutely abolished."[13]

And it is no wonder that indulgences were so sought after by the people of the day, for the teaching of *purgatory* kept them in constant fear and dread of their own death, and caused those bereaved of loved ones untold pain and misery in the contemplation of their sufferings. Space does not permit a full recounting of people's concepts and beliefs about purgatory,[14] but a few of the accounts and stories should be introduced so that the reader can get a grasp of the fear that the vast majority of Roman Catholics had, *and many still have,* concerning purgatory.

F.X. Shouppe recounts one of many stories:

> "In the year 1589, in the monastery of St. Mary of the Angels, in Florence, died a Religious who was much esteemed by her sisters in religion, but who soon appeared to St. Magdalen de Pazzi to implore her assistance in the rigorous Purgatory to which she was condemned. The saint was in prayer before the Blessed Sacrament when she perceived the deceased kneeling in the middle of the church in an attitude of profound adoration. She had around her a mantle of flames that seemed to consume her, but a white robe that covered her body protected her in part from the action of the fire. Greatly aston-

> ished, Magdalen desired to know what this signified, and she was answered that this soul suffered thus for having had little devotion toward the August Sacrament of the Altar. Notwithstanding the rules and holy customs of her Order, she had communicated but rarely, and then with indifference. It was for this reason Divine Justice had condemned her to come every day to adore the Blessed Sacrament, and to submit to the torture of fire at the feet of Jesus Christ. Nevertheless, in reward for her virginal purity, represented by the white robe, her Divine Spouse had greatly mitigated her sufferings.
>
> "Such was the revelation which God made to His servant. She was deeply touched, and made every effort to assist the poor soul by all the suffrages in her power. She often related this apparition, and made use of it to exhort her spiritual daughters to zeal for Holy Communion."[15]

William Cathcart provides some chilling examples of the stories circulated amongst the people concerning purgatory. One he cites from Bede's "Ecclesiastical History" concerning a man who died, but came back to life again, and recounted this story:

> "'He that led me,' says he, 'had a shining countenance and a white garment; he brought me to a vale full of dreadful flames on the left; the side horrid for violent hail and cold snow; both places were full of men's souls, which seemed to be tossed

> by an angry storm from one side to the other; for when the wretches could no longer endure the violent heat, they leaped into the chilling cold, and finding no rest there they bounded back again into the unquenchable flames. It became densely dark, and my leader forsook me, and I observed frequent globes of black flames rising out of a great pit and falling back into it; and the flames as they ascended were full of human souls, like sparks flying up with smoke, which dropped down into the depths below when the vapor of the fire ceased.
>
> "On a sudden I heard the noise of hideous lamentation, and the loud laughter of a rude multitude insulting captured enemies; it was a gang of evil spirits dragging the howling and lamenting souls of men, whilst they themselves were laughing and rejoicing. They went down into the midst of the pit of fire until I could no longer distinguish between the lamentation of the men and the laughter of the devils. Some of the dark spirits ascended from the flaming abyss, and beset me on all sides with their glaring eyes, and the stench of the fire which proceeded from their mouths and nostrils. They threatened to seize me with burning tongs, when my guide appeared and put them to flight, and took me into a sense of great light and happiness.'"[16]

The man went on to explain that the souls he had seen were there so that they might amend and confess their sins, and that many were helped by the prayers and alms of the living, and especially by the masses.

For the Christian, the whole concept of merits, satisfactions, sufferings, etc., seems so foreign, so far from the believer's experience of the full sufficiency of Jesus Christ and the *complete* and full forgiveness of sins that is found in Him (and in Him alone), that it is difficult, if one is not a former Roman Catholic, to begin to conceive of the dread that can take hold upon a person's soul when faced with the near certainty of purgatory. Add to this the fact that *the RCC has never defined just how long a time can be spent in purgatory.* The people at the time of the Reformation believed it could literally be millennia—thousands of years—before finding release from the sufferings of that place. Is it any wonder that people flocked to the Tetzels of the day, buying for themselves, and for loved ones, release from such horrid punishment?

The RCC doesn't sell indulgences anymore, but the theology that underlies indulgences and purgatory is alive and well in Rome. The Vatican II Council decreed:

> "This most sacred Synod accepts with great devotion the venerable faith of our ancestors regarding this vital fellowship with our brethren who are in heavenly glory or who are still being purified after death. It proposes again the decrees of the Second Council of Nicea, the Council of Florence, and the Council of Trent."[17]

Hence, the Roman Catholic is still taught that a place of "purging" exists where souls suffer, and in so doing, make satisfaction for the "stains of sin" still on their souls. Not only this, but the whole doctrine of indulgences is discussed, and re-affirmed, in Paul VI's

"Indulgentiarum Doctrina" of January 1, 1967. The Pope's document began,

> "1. The doctrine of indulgences and their practice have been in force for many centuries in the Catholic Church. They would appear to be solidly founded on divine Revelation, handed down 'from the apostles.' This (tradition (sic)' ...makes progress in the Church, with the help of the Holy Spirit,' and 'as the centuries go by, the Church is always advancing towards the plenitude of divine truth, until eventually the words of God are fulfilled in her.'"[18]

The Pope goes on to reaffirm that "expiation must be made in the next life through fire and torments or *purifying* punishments,"[19] and goes on to say,

> "The doctrine of purgatory clearly demonstrates that even when the guilt of sin has been taken away, punishment for it or the consequences of it may remain to be expiated or cleansed. They often are. In fact, in purgatory the souls of those 'who died in the charity of God and truly repentant, but who had not made satisfaction with adequate penance for their sins and omissions' are cleansed after death with punishments designed to purge away their debt."[20]

Surely the *theology* of purgatory and indulgences has not changed in Romanism.

To summarize, then, it should be remembered that

according to the Roman teaching, just as was seen in the doctrine of the sacrifice of the Mass, when sin is "forgiven" this "forgiveness" does not always remit the temporal punishments of sin, and indeed it frequently does not. Souls that die in a state of sanctifying grace (which would involve, as a bare minimum, baptism) go to purgatory if they have any "stain of sin" upon them. This would include venial sins, and their temporal punishment, as well as the temporal punishment of mortal sins forgiven in confession. By their suffering in purgatory, these punishments are satisfied, or, as Ludwig Ott put it, by the "suffering of atonement" they are purged. These "poor souls" can be aided by the living on earth through prayers, masses, acts of mercy, etc., and by the application of indulgences to them. These indulgences, drawing from the "treasury of merit," are able to remit temporal punishments for the living, and reduce (it is believed) the time spent in purgatory by the departed. This "treasury of merit" assumes that the Virgin Mary and the saints had "excess merit" of their own, and that there is merit in Christ's death that is "exeess," which the RCC then can apply as it sees fit.

So we have seen the Roman doctrine of the Mass and purgatory, and what the RCC teaches, as revealed in these doctrines, concerning sin and salvation, justification and the work of Jesus Christ. This writer surely rejects nearly everything that Rome has taught in these doctrines. But why? On what basis? We shall now turn to the Bible, God's written revelation to man, and ask the question, "what does the Bible teach about salvation, and especially about the work of Jesus Christ?" We will look at the basic doctrines of God's sovereignty, man's inability, God's free and effective grace seen in election and regeneration, and the perseverance of God's people in their holy living. Then we will look with particular care at the work of Jesus Christ on the Cross, keeping in mind what we have learned of the Roman doctrines. So, let us now turn from dogmatic pronouncements to the divine Word, from conciliar decisions to the testimony of the Holy Spirit in the Word of God, the Bible, for as Isaiah said long ago:

"To the law and to the testimony! If they do not speak according to this word, there is no dawn in them!" (Isaiah 8:20)

Chapter 5
The Gospel of the Grace of God in Jesus Christ

The Christian message of salvation in the Gospel differs *fundamentally* from the teachings of Roman Catholicism. It is not simply a matter of *differing interpretations or theological subtleties*; the differences are of such a foundational, basic nature that it is simply impossible for *both* to be "true." At nearly every point the Biblical teachings about man, sin, regeneration, forgiveness, justification, and sanctification are misrepresented by the Roman system in its effort to maintain a doctrinal structure that has developed and evolved over a thousand years and more. Unfortunately, that development was not guided or limited by the revelation of God in the Scriptures. Instead, the Scriptures were subjugated to the authority of the Roman Church.[1]

The resultant teachings of Rome do not share the Bible's basic viewpoint of the Gospel: God-centeredness. The Biblical Gospel begins with God, is carried out by God, ends with God, and results in God's glory. Man does not begin his salvation, does not deserve salvation, cannot even begin to merit forgiveness for spitting on the sidewalk, let alone for any other sin, is spiritually dead and enslaved to evil, is unable to come to Christ outside of the Father's effective and powerful drawing, continues after his regeneration to be utterly and completely dependent upon the Spirit of God and the grace of God for all he is or ever shall be, and shall continue in that state into eternity itself. The Bible does not present God as one who *hopes* to save, or just *wants* to save, but is hampered—no, utterly frustrated in a large portion of the cases—by the almighty will of the creature, man. The God of Scripture is *powerful to save*, and when He sets His lovingkindness upon a person, and intends to bring that person to glory, He shall never, ever fail of His goal.

We looked briefly at some of the concepts involved in the Roman view of salvation, such things as the definition of *sin, justification*, and the *sacraments*. To look at the Biblical perspective, we will need to step back even farther and look at some very foundational concepts involving *the nature of God, the effect of sin on man, and God's electing grace*. These items need to be reviewed for three reasons: first, any discussion of such things as atonement, righteousness, sanctification, etc., must be based upon the more basic elements of who God is and how God does things to be in any way meaningful; secondly, the Roman Catholic must understand *how and why* the Christian Gospel differs so fundamentally from that which he or she has been taught; and thirdly, the Christian of today may not have been challenged to think through his beliefs about the Gospel, and hence may hold to certain concepts that are antithetical to a solid understanding of Biblical teaching.

The Sovereignty of God

The Psalmist could say, "Our God is in heaven; He does whatever pleases Him" (Psalm 115:3). Modern men often laugh at such a view of God, but it would seem that they will find themselves the object of His laughter in the final analysis. The unanimous testimony of sacred Scripture is that God is sovereign, He is in control of all that takes place within His creation. "Everything which pleases Yahweh He does in the heavens and on earth, in the seas and all their depths" (Psalm 135:6). This was the faith of Israel. God, as Creator of all that exists, *must* then rule over the works of His hands, and that with wisdom and justice. The universe does not spin about, directed only by fate. Rather, it is directed by the hand of God Himself. "And you are My witnesses, says Yahweh, that I am God. Even from eternity I am He—who can deliver out of My hand? I act, and who can reverse it?" (Isaiah 43:12-13). "I make light and create darkness, I make peace and create disaster; I, Yahweh, do all these things" (Isaiah 45:7). "I make known the end from the beginning, from ancient times, and what is yet to come. I say, My purpose will stand, and I will do all that I desire" (Isaiah 46:10). It is readily admitted that such high views of God and His providence in the world are rare in much of what calls itself "Christianity" today. Many are fearful of openly confessing such a belief in God, for to do so surely results in a view of man that is not popular! A God such as the One who speaks through Isaiah is not wanted when men look to themselves as the center of the universe, the most important beings in existence. As long as man thinks himself *indepenent* of God, the message of God's absolute sovereignty will not be welcome.

But the Scriptures present man as existing under the guiding hand of God. This is directly stated more than once by the writer of Proverbs: "Many are the plans in the heart of a man, but it is Yahweh's purpose that will prevail" (Proverbs 19:21); "From Yahweh are the steps of a man; how can man understand his way?"

(Proverbs 20:24); "Like a water-course in the hand of Yahweh is the king's heart: He directs it where He pleases" (Proverbs 21:1). But we are not limited to Proverbs for our basis of this truth! Did not God tell Abimelech that He, the Lord, had *kept him from sinning* in the matter of Sarah in Genesis 20:6? How can *God keep a man from sinning* if it is not in His power to do so? And, if He could keep Abimelech from sinning, could He not also *keep everyone* from sinning *if it were His will*? God's control even over the *desires* of man can be seen in the promise to the Israelites in Exodus 34:24. Here, the Law commands that three times a year the men of the nation are to appear before the Lord. But, how could this be? Does not God know that the Israelites are surrounded on every side by pagan peoples who wish only to destroy them? How could the men leave their families and lands unprotected? A promise is given along with the commandment, a promise which *demands* a very high view of God! Yahweh says, "...and no one will covet (desire) your land when you go up three times to appear before Yahweh your God."

That men's hearts are not restricted from the rulership of God can be seen in many other instances as well. Deuteronomy 2:30 tells us that with reference to the king of Heshbon God *made his spirit stubborn and his heart hard or obstinate*. And for what reason? So that the Lord could deliver him into the hands of the Israelites. A similar action on the part of God is to be found in Joshua 11:20. Many centuries later God would use the Assyrians as "the rod of my anger" against the sinful Israelites, though that surely was not what the Assyrians had in mind (Isaiah 10:5-7)! They were doing what they were doing simply because it was their evil nature to do so. Yet, God was so using their evil desires *to accomplish His own Holy will*.

Examples such as these could, quite truly, be multiplied indefinitely.[2] The writers of the New Testament surely believed in this view of God as strongly as the writers of the Old. Paul could describe God as "the one who works out all things according to the intention of His will" in Ephesians 1:11. We will see, specifically in regard to God's election, that the New Testament is full of God's sovereign grace, but one example will suffice to demonstrate to any honest reader the fact that God is not only sovereign over all the actions of men, but that He has also willed to use the *evil actions of men to His glory*.

No one can doubt that the sacrifice of Jesus Christ on the cross of Calvary was God's intention from eternity past. The cross was no mistake, but was central to the very purpose for which Christ came. As the Lord Himself stated, no one took His life from Him, but He laid it down of His own accord (John 10:18). It was the purpose of God that Jesus Christ die as the substitute for sinners, taking their place, bearing their guilt, their punishment, upon Himself, so that they might become the righteousness of God in Him (2 Corinthians 5:21). It also cannot be argued that the action of crucifying Christ, including His treatment and condemnation at the hands of Herod, Pilate, and the Jewish leaders, was not sinful in the extreme. Putting the sinless Son of God to death is an action of such horrid depravity and wickedness as to almost defy description. Yet, in Acts chapter 4, the Church gathers to pray to God, and they say,

> "For truly in this city there were gathered together against your Holy Child Jesus whom you anointed, Herod and Pontius Pilate together with the Gentiles and the people of Israel, to *do whatever your hand and purpose predestined to take place*."

Here the early Church confesses her faith in the sovereign and guiding hand of God, even in the wicked action of putting her Lord to death! From the human perspective only, the cross was a terrible evil, so how could it be said that God had predestined that this evil take place? And yet from God's perspective, revealed to us in His Word, we understand that *no other action in history will bring so much glory to God as the work of Christ upon Calvary*. Even when we cannot see the ultimate outcome of glory and good, we can be confident that such will indeed be the case, no matter how dark or evil the actions of men.

Why is it important to have a proper perspective on the sovereignty of God? Salvation is the work of God, wherein He brings sinful man into a right relationship with Himself. Just about every single false teaching on salvation finds its basis, its origin, in one of two ideas, which are not really two, but simply different aspects of one falsehood. These ideas are, 1) a denial of the sovereignty of God, and 2) a false view of the abilities of man in sin. Man does not wish to confess the sovereignty of God, for to do so is to admit one's own dependence and subjection to God. Nothing is farther from the sinful heart of man than belief in the sovereignty of God. Even the saints themselves, guided and directed by the Spirit of God, often have trouble accepting and living with the sovereignty of God. If you wish to see the depth of the hatred of man for God—the *real* God of the Bible who sits upon His throne and rules and reigns—simply assert the divine authority of God over the life of each and every human being! The vile hatred will overflow, and you will be mocked and ridiculed for being so "narrow" or so "self-righteous." It is far more "comfortable" for men to view God as the "great Responder" in the sky, who is busily engaged in *respond-*

ing to men, meeting their needs, but never *ruling* or directing. Yet, no proper understanding of the Gospel of Christ can be based on anything other than the Biblical view of God Himself. Any teaching of the Gospel that compromises or denies the eternal sovereignty of the Almighty God will not be true to Scripture.

We can see how this is relevant to the Roman Catholic perspective, which views God as providing "cooperating" grace to all men, yet the final determination is still up to men, not God. But most of modern evangelicalism is in no better shape. It is frightening to see how easily and quickly the sovereignty of God is jettisoned in favor of a Gospel presentation that is more *acceptable* to man. We don't want to offend anyone, and preaching God's sovereignty and man's dependence is surely repugnant to unconverted men. Yes, it is, and so it should be! But it is no less true for being offensive! The yardstick of truth for the Gospel is not men's approval of it, but whether it is consistent with the revelation of God in Scripture. C.H. Spurgeon expressed it well:

> "There is no attribute more comforting to His children than that of God's Sovereignty. Under the most adverse circumstances, in the most severe trials, they believe that Sovereignty has ordained their afflictions, that Sovereignty overrules them, and that Sovereignty will sanctify them all...On the other hand, there is no doctrine more hated by worldlings, no truth of which they have made such a football, as the great, stupendous, but yet most certain doctrine of the Sovereignty of the infinite Jehovah. Men will allow God to be everywhere except on His throne.

> They will allow Him to be in His workshop to fashion worlds and make stars. They will allow Him to be in His almonry to dispense His alms and bestow His bounties. They will allow Him to sustain the earth and bear up the pillars thereof, or light the lamps of heaven, or rule the waves of the evermoving ocean; but when God ascends His throne, His creatures gnash their teeth, and we proclaim an enthroned God, and His right to do as He wills with His own, to dispose of His creatures as He thinks well, without consulting them in the matter; then it is that we are hissed and execrated, and then it is that men turn a deaf ear to us, for God on His throne is not the God they love. But it is God upon the throne that we love to preach. It is God upon His throne whom we trust."[3]

Today's Christians need to go back and take a good look at the God of the Bible, and, if they do, they will be shocked at the *vast difference* between the God of Scripture and the God of Madison Avenue that is preached from so many pulpits.[4]

The Roman Catholic Church does not directly deny the concept of God's sovereignty. However, in practice and doctrine, particularly in regards to salvation, the *logical outworking* of God's sovereign nature is seriously compromised. Not only this, but much of the "gospel preaching" that is directed *at* Roman Catholicism is ineffective, for it *too* denies the practical ramifications of a belief in the God of Scripture. The presentation of the work of God found, for example, in many popular books of today is not going to be able to properly address

Roman teachings and doctrine, for it partakes of many of the same misconceptions about God, sin, and grace.

Man in his sin

We noted above that the farthest thing from the heart of the unregenerate man is an acknowledgement, in truth, of the sovereignty of God. This is not to say that people may not *affirm* such a belief for this reason or that, but to *live it* and to truly bow before **the** Holy God revealed in Scripture is another issue. Why is this? Why are men bent on denying the truth of God and His Word?

The answer lies in the nature of man as *sinner.* Sin is rebellion against God. Frequently the Scriptures speak of it as "lawlessness" and this is surely to be understood as a rebellion not against the *law* so much as the *Lawgiver* Himself, the Lord God. The Apostle Paul gave us the classic passage on the nature and effects of sin in his epistle to the Romans, chapter 1, verses 18 and following. In part we read,

> "For the wrath of God is revealed from heaven against all ungodliness and unrighteousness of men, who suppress the truth in unrighteousness, for what is known of God is made manifest in them, for God manifested it to them. For His invisible things (His eternal power and divine nature) have been seen since the creation of the world, being understood through what has been made, so that they have no excuse. For though they knew God they did not glorify Him as God or give thanks, but they became futile in their reasonings and their foolish hearts were made dark. Professing themselves to be

> wise, they were made fools, and they exchanged the glory of the incorruptible God for corruptible human images, and birds and animals and reptiles. Therefore God delivered them over in the desires of their hearts to uncleanness to dishonor their bodies amongst themselves. These exchanged the truth of God for the lie, and worshiped and served the created things rather than the Creator, who is blessed forever, amen."

Something of the horrid nature of sin, and its terrible effect upon man, can be seen from these words. Basic to Paul's understanding of sin is the *twisting of the Creator/creation relationship*. Paul says that man, in rebellion against God, denies the real nature of God. Though man knows of God's existence, he does not glorify God or give thanks to Him. We have been asked many times by atheists, "why should I praise God? Any God who would want to be praised must be sick!" Yet, it is clear from what Paul says that man recognizes that if God exists, God is worthy of praise and thanks. But man refuses to recognize this God, for to do so would be to give up man's most precious possession: *his own independence, his own autonomy*. Man in sin "flip-flops" reality: instead of recognizing himself as the created being, and God as his Creator, he places himself in the position of the "supreme being" and, in his incredible arrogance, assumes he can sit in judgment upon God. If God does something man doesn't like, he just rejects that God exists, or that God wills this or that. Rebellion. A denial of the real nature of God. It is at the center of man's sin. It is a part of every sin-stained heart. We hold to our self-proclaimed independence of God with every bit of our strength, every fiber of our being. Outside of the omnipotent strength of the Spirit of God, no man would ever give up that rebellion, that denial of who God truly is.

Modern philosophical notions such as humanism have infected the thinking of Christians so deeply that we are afraid to proclaim the Bible's own view of man. Thankfully, Paul did not give in to such pressures, and frankly described man in his sin:

> "Just as it has been written,
> There is none righteous, not even one,
> There is none who understands,
> There is none who seeks after God.
> All have turned away, together they have become worthless,
> There is none who does good, not even one.
> Their throats are open graves,
> their tongues deceive,
> the poison of asps is on their lips.
> Their mouths are full of cursing and bitterness,
> Their feet are swift to shed blood,
> And the way of peace they have not known.
> There is no fear of God before their eyes."
> (Romans 3:10-18)

Here is a test for the believer: will these words of Scripture be taken seriously, and their teaching accepted, or will we, in our rebellion and pride, reject them? Paul obviously did not feel that these passages were unimportant, for his discussion of man's sinfulness takes up nearly three full chapters *prior* to his discussion of salvation. Obviously, the Apostle felt that the message of man's condition in sin was *basic and foundational* to a proper understanding of justification, forgiveness, etc. Paul's words cannot be ignored. He says that there is *none who is righteous, none who understands, none who does good.* This means that anyone who is righteous is righteous only because God makes them so; anyone who understands understands only because God has revealed it to them, anyone who does good does so because God is working through them. Note also that the Bible says that "there is none who seeks after God." The Greek text has "there is one who seeks after God," with the strong negative "NOT" put right at the beginning to negate the whole phrase. *"There is no such thing as a God-seeker!"* Yet, Romanism speaks of men "preparing themselves" or "converting themselves" and much of modern evangelicalism speaks in the same way, assuming that there are many who are "seeking after God" and all one has to do is tell them about Jesus and all will be well. But Paul says there are no God seekers! And how could there be? The same Apostle said elsewhere, "And you, **being dead in your trespasses and sins**..." (Ephesians 2:1). Man in his sin is spiritually dead. Dead men do not seek after God. Dead men don't seek after anything, actually. Dead men are dead. Just how seriously the Bible's teaching on the deadness of man in sin is taken will determine much of what a person will believe about salvation. Few are those who are willing to openly tell people that there is nothing, absolutely nothing, they can do to save themselves. They are utterly and completely dependent upon God for their salvation. What a shattering blow to man's pride! What a crushing shot at man's self-esteem! But the person who realizes that, outside of God's intervention and grace, there would be no chance for him, no way of salvation in Christ, is the one in whom God has already begun to work. True faith, which looks to Christ alone, will be found in such a person as the result of God's giving it. Anyone who is truly seeking God is doing so only because God has chosen them and is drawing them to Himself. Outside of this action of God, no man will come to Christ.

Is this not what Jesus Himself taught? In John 6:44, when speaking to the crowd, Jesus said, "No man is able to come to Me unless the Father, who sent Me, draws him, and I will raise him up at the last day." The Lord did not say *"no man will want to come to Me..."* though that is true; rather, He used a term of *ability* when He said "no man **is able to come** to Me, unless the Father draws him..." Why is this? Answered simply, man is spiritually dead, and coming to Christ requires spiritual life. Paul explained it like this:

> "But the natural man does not receive the things of the Spirit of God, for they are foolishness to him, and *neither is he able to know them*, for they are spiritually discerned." (I Corinthians 2:14).

The "natural man," the man who is not spiritual, who has not been raised from the condition of spiritual death to that of spiritual life,[5] simply will not come to Christ, for he is unable to do so. Since all men are in this condition, then, it is obvious that salvation is the work of God and God alone. Outside of God's *first* moving in a person's life, there can be no salvation. And note as well in passing that this "drawing" spoken of in John 6:44 is not some nebulous, general drawing that can be taken or left by the individual, but a *specific and effective* drawing, which *always* results in salvation, for as the Lord Jesus said, all who are drawn will be raised up by Him at the last day—another way of referring to salvation.[6]

The Bible is clear: man outside of Christ is unable to do good, to seek God, to understand the things of God.

Jeremiah asked long ago, "Can the Ethiopian change his skin or the leopard its spots? Neither can you do good who are used to doing evil" (Jeremiah 13:23). He knew that the human heart is "deceitful above all things and beyond cure" (Jeremiah 17:9). Man's total nature—his mind, his intellect, his will—has been corrupted by sin. As a result, man is totally dependent upon the grace of God, not simply to "enable him to cooperate" with that grace, but to bring him spiritual life, to enable him *to do anything at all.*

So why do we not hear more of these Biblical teachings today? If one takes the sovereignty of God seriously, and the depravity of man seriously, there is only one possible answer to the question of salvation: God saves without the aid or assistance of man. Man's pride is sorely bruised by this fact. We wish to have a part in "saving ourselves" so that we might in some way boast before God. But we have no place for such boasting. God has saved us. All the glory belongs to Him. Such a teaching, we recognize, is anathematized by Roman Catholicism.[7] But the anathemas of men's councils are of little importance compared to the teaching of the Word of God.

A word should be said concerning the seriousness of sin. It is imbedded deep in the heart of every man: a horrid ability to down-play sin and its effects, and to ignore, if at all possible, a reality that frightens us to the core of our being. *If the God of Scripture exists as He reveals Himself in those pages*, then sin—no matter how "trivial" or "venial" it might seem to us—**any sin**, is worthy of the most strict and grievous punishment. Why? The thrice-holy God of the Bible is the one against whom we sin. It is He who sits enthroned in His temple, surrounded by the seraphim, those holy angels, who even themselves, spotless as they are, unstained by sin, cannot bear to look at His majesty, but cover their faces with their wings (Isaiah 6:2). From these mighty creatures comes the confession that every man, upon looking at the true God, must make: "Holy! Holy! Holy is Yahweh of Hosts! The whole earth is full of His glory!" Can we ever begin to really comprehend what it is to flaunt the law and will of such a Being? Can any punishment be too severe for sinning against such a Holy One's honor? The person who thinks it strange that man should be punished for his sin knows neither God nor his own heart.

Since this is so, it naturally follows that *no action of sinful man can have the least value in God's sight with reference to the forgiveness of sin.* It is an infinite God who is offended by sin. Shall we be so presumptuous, so foolish, to think that any human action could even *begin* to make satisfaction for such a heinous crime? An infinite God requires an infinite satisfaction for the infinite punishment against the sin that has slighted His infinite honor. It is for this reason that one can only stand before God *robed in the righteousness of Jesus Christ and Him alone, for even our righteous acts are as filthy rags in His sight* (Isaiah 64:6). The greatest suffering, the greatest works, are nothing but filth in the eyes of the Holy God. Is there one of us who is so arrogant, so dishonest, as to say that *even the motivations of our good works are totally pure*? So how can we pretend that these good works have merit in God's sight? The more we know of God, the more we come to understand His holiness and justice, the less we will think of our own goodness, and the more we will recognize our utter helplessness and our total dependence upon His grace and His grace alone.

Distinctions in Sin?

What of the Roman Catholic teaching that there are

different "classes" of sin, venial and mortal, with differing punishments attached? Such a concept, surely, comes from both a very low view of the holiness of God as well as a very flawed view of sin itself. What can possibly be "venial" in sin? What rebellion against the Creator can be considered "lesser" than another? Surely we recognize that from man's perspective, it is far worse to murder than to swear falsely. Yet, we must realize that both are deserving of death before the Holy God of heaven. Both blaspheme His name and His glory. It is easy to dismiss a "venial" sin as something that is not serious, for is it not taught that one does not even need to confess the venial sins to the priest? A few "Hail Marys" and all will be well. Such a teaching provides an excuse for secret sin and rebellion against God, and fosters the idea that God sits in heaven "winking" at the "less serious" sins of man, when the truth is that Christ died for *all the sins of God's people*. The "venial" sin requires the blood of Christ for remission just as any other.

And what of the concept of temporal punishments remaining after forgiveness in Christ? John Calvin answered this fully:

> "This is the new covenant that God in Christ has made with us, that he will remember our sins no more [Jer. 31:31, 34]. What he meant by these words we learn from another prophet, where the Lord says: 'If a righteous man turns away from his righteousness,...I will not remember his righteous deeds" [Ezek. 18:24 p.]; 'if a wicked man turns away from his impiety, I will not remember his sins' [Ezek. 18:21-22 p.; cf v.27]. His statement that he will not remember their

> righteous acts means virtually this: he will not keep an account of them to reward them. The statement that he will not remember their sins therefore means that he will not demand the penalty for them. The same thing is said elsewhere: 'Cast...behind my back' [Isa. 38:17]; 'swept away like a cloud' [Isa. 44:22]; 'cast...into the depths of the sea' [Micah 7:19]; 'not to reckon it to his account and keep it hidden' [cf. Ps. 32:1-2]. By such expressions the Holy Spirit clearly would have explained his meaning to us, if we had listened to them attentively. Surely, if God punishes sins, he charges them to our account; if he takes vengeance, he remembers them; if he calls to judgment, he does not hide them; if he weighs them, he has not cast them behind his back; if he scrutinizes them, he has not blotted them out like a cloud; if he airs them, he has not cast them into the depths of the sea."[8]

The *completeness of forgiveness* that is promised by God in Christ refutes any possibility of the continuing punishment of sin, for the sinner is not simply *paroled* but he is **pardoned**. If the sin, then, is forgiven, God has no basis upon which to punish. It cannot be argued that God's "justice demands punishment" as Christ was punished in our place. As Calvin went on to say,

> "What, I ask you, would Christ have bestowed upon us if the penalty for our sins were still required? For when we say that he bore all our sins in his body upon

> the tree [I Peter 2:24], we mean only that he bore the punishment and vengeance due for our sins. Isaiah has stated this more meaningfully when he says: 'The chastisement (or correction) of our peace was upon him' [Isa. 53:5]. What is this 'correction of our peace' but the penalty due sins that we would have had to pay before we could become reconciled to God—if he had not taken our place?"[9]

Therefore we see that the Roman concept of temporal punishment remaining after the forgiveness of our sins in Jesus Christ is out of harmony with the Biblical teaching of the fullness of the atoning work of Christ. More concerning the completeness of Christ's work, and its wonderful application to the soul of the sinner, will be said below.

The Unconditional Electing Grace of God

If all men are dead in sin, utterly incapable of the first movement toward the Holy God, but instead are intent upon denying Him and His right as Creator, who then can be saved? Only the one who is the object of God's sovereign and free grace. The sole difference between the person who is lost for eternity and the saint in glory is the grace of God and absolutely nothing else. No man deserves even the notice of God let alone His mercy and grace. There is nothing in the creature man that *draws* the mercy of God, nothing that makes God take notice of one man over another. All are alike condemned and worthy of damnation. Yet, He has saved men. Why? We can look only to the glorious grace of God in Christ Jesus for the answer to that question. He saved simply because He willed to do so. It is His right to do with His creation as He pleases, and He was pleased to show mercy and grace to some, deserved justice and wrath to others.

We cannot count the number of times that people of various religious backgrounds—Mormons, Roman Catholics, liberal Protestants—have replied to our statement of the above truth of God, "If that is what God is like, I don't want Him!" Man hates the fact that, outside of God's grace and mercy, he is utterly helpless, simply the *creation* of God, not God's co-equal. But such responses, natural as they are from the heart of the sinner, ignore the truth of God's sovereign being, His absolute Kingship over all the universe. Those attitudes also do not take sin and its enormity in God's sight with proper seriousness. Others might say, "but that simply is not what the Bible teaches!" Let us look to Scripture and see.

Let us begin with the Master Himself, the Lord Jesus Christ. We will listen His words in the synagogue at Capernaum in John 6. Many Roman Catholics look to this passage as evidence of Jesus' teaching that it is necessary to literally "eat His flesh" and "drink His blood" to gain salvation, claiming that this is in fact a prophecy of the establishment of the Eucharist. But, as the text clearly shows, this is a gross misunderstanding. Christ Jesus most definitely does discuss salvation here, but His words carry a very different meaning. We will look closely at this passage:

> 37. Everyone which the Father gives to Me will come to Me, and the one coming to Me I will never cast out 38. because I have come from heaven not in order that I might do My will but the will of Him who sent Me; 39. and this is the will of the one who sent Me: that of all which He has given Me from Him I lose nothing but raise

it up at the last day.

This section continues the thought brought out in verse 36. Jesus presents the complete sovereignty of God in salvation. All that the Father gives to Jesus—everyone—will come to Him. The operative factor in answering the question of why some come and others, presented with the same opportunity, do not, is simply the nature of the Father's choice. The Father "gives" persons to the Son—a gift of love, to be sure. When the Father "gives" to the Son a person, that person will come to Christ (as the one avenue to the Father). There is no question that if a person is so given to Christ (or, to use the terminology of verse 44, is so "drawn" by the Father) that he/she will come to Christ. This is the "Godward" side of salvation —absolute certainty and security. Yet, He says that they will "come to Me" which speaks of the human response—not that the human can change the decision of God—but that the response is there all the same. Man is not pictured simply as a "thing" that is bounced around like a ball, but rather a vastly important person who comes to Christ for salvation, all as the result of the gracious working of God in his/her life. Jesus continues by stating that when one is so given to Him by the Father, and comes to Him, that one is secure in his relationship with Him—He will never cast them out. The Greek phrase used here is very strong,[10] and indicates that rejection of one who seeks refuge in Christ is a complete and total impossibility. What words to a sinner's heart! Those who come to Christ will find Him a loving Lord who will never cast out those who trust in Him!

Why will the Lord never cast out those who come to Him? Verse 38 continues the thought with an explanation—the Son has come to do the will of the Father. And what is the will of the Father? That "of all which He has given Me from Him I lose nothing but raise it up at the last day." Can we doubt that Christ will do what He promises? Will the Lord Jesus ever fail to do the Father's will? Here is eternal security beyond dispute. But note that again all is pre-eminently balanced—the security of the person is based on two things—the will of the Father that none be lost, and secondly, the fact that those who are not lost are those who are given to the Son by the Father Himself. So, in reality, there is security in the Father (He gives us to Christ) and security in the Son (He always does the Father's will).

> 40. For this is the will of My Father: that all the ones looking upon the Son and believing in Him might have eternal life and I will raise him up at the last day."

The "will of the Father" for the Son was expressed in verse 39; now, the "will of the Father" is expressed differently. Again, the perfect and complete balance of God's role and man's response is brought forward. In verse 39 is the assurance of the Son's success in saving those given to Him by the Father. In verse 40 is the promise that all the ones looking upon the Son and believing in Him might have eternal life. It is evident that many look upon the Son but do not believe; the operative difference was the drawing (or "enablement") of the Father. Here it is clear that the "all" refers to those mentioned in the immediate context—all those whom the Father has given to the Son. For them, it is the looking and believing that brings eternal life. The Father's drawing is to them invisible—they see only Christ.

It should be noted that it is exceptionally high "doctrine" that is here presented. Isn't this out of place? One would expect this kind of teaching in Ephesians, or maybe Philippians, or might expect it to be more at home in Calvin's *Institutes*—but amongst a crowd of Galileans in the synagogue at Capernaum? Is it any wonder that the people found these sayings "hard to hear"? Why then the "high doctrine"? I feel that the response of the men on a purely physical plane to the spiritual teachings of Christ, demonstrated by their inability to get past the physical symbol and penetrate to the spiritual reality, prompted an explanation on Jesus' part. Why do people respond to His words and His works in such different ways? Jesus is not seeking followers on the level they are pursuing—they need to know the truth of His mission. Those whom the Father leaves in their darkness will respond to Christ in very different ways than those who have been given to Him by the Father. It is time to separate the true disciples from the false—the called from the whimsically interested. "High doctrine" is nothing more than the truth at its purest. It is meant for the peasant farmer as well as the theologian.

> 41. Therefore the Jews were grumbling concerning Him, because He said, "I am the bread which came down out of heaven."
> 42. And they said, "Is this not Jesus, the Son of Joseph? Do we not know His father and His mother? Therefore how does He say "I came down out of heaven?"

The human reaction of the crowd is not surprising. Jesus' claims finally begin to sink in, though they seem to be running a little behind the Lord's message! They grumble because of His claim to heavenly origin. Their questions are straightforward—isn't this Jesus, the son of Joseph? They knew the family of the Lord; Joseph and Mary were known in the synagogue of Capernaum.

Thinking in strictly human terms (not understanding John's own statement of the Word becoming flesh, the dual nature of the Lord) how could this one whose parents we know claim to "come down out of heaven"?

> 43. Jesus answered and said unto them, "Do not grumble among yourselves! 44. No one is able to come to Me unless the Father who sent Me draws him, and I will raise him up at the last day.

Jesus brushes aside the grumbling and objections of the crowd by pinpointing their inability to accept His claims about Himself. In even stronger terms He reiterates that which He has said before: no one has the ability in and of themselves to come to Him unless the Father draws him. This is here expressed by Jesus as the reason the people are unable to understand or accept His divine origin. Absolutely necessary is the "drawing" of the Father. The term "drawing" is used elsewhere in John of Jesus drawing all to Himself when He is lifted up (John 12:32—though here it is Jesus who does the drawing) and at the end of the gospel when Peter "drags" the net full of fishes onto the shore. It is impossible to maintain a "universal" drawing here, for all who are drawn are also raised up. The Father draws, and the Son raises up those who are drawn. This is exactly parallel to verses 37-39 above, only in more stark terms. Here we have election on a par with Ephesians 1 and Romans 8-9.

This is certainly not the only passage where the Lord Jesus presents these truths. Matthew 11:27 presents the same concepts, only is shorter expression. When one grasps the truth that no man can come to Christ unless the Father draws him, and that the Father has *not* drawn all indiscriminately, the reactions of the crowds to Jesus' teachings become understandable—whether there by the Sea of Galilee or today on a street corner in America. You can proclaim the exact same message to two different people, and get two utterly different reactions. Why? One is met with faith, for God grants spiritual life and faith to that individual. The other responds with unbelief. The sole difference lies in the Father's choice.

The Lord left it to His Apostles to draw this teaching out with greater clarity, and this was done primarily by Paul. Numerous passages from Paul teach the truths spoken by the Lord in John 6. When writing to the Thessalonians Paul said, "We ought to give thanks to God always for you, brethren loved by the Lord, for God chose you from the beginning for salvation through sanctification by the Spirit and faith in the truth" (2 Thessalonians 2:13). And in writing to his beloved Timothy he taught, "He saved us, and called us with a holy calling, not on the basis of our works, but according to His own purpose and grace, which was given to us in Christ Jesus before the beginning of time" (2 Timothy 1:9). But the clearest presentations of the elective grace of God are to be found in the opening chapter of the book of Ephesians and in the 8th and 9th chapters of his epistle to the Romans.

> "Blessed be the God and Father of our Lord Jesus Christ, who blessed us with every spiritual blessing in the heavenly places in Christ, just as He chose us in Him before the foundation of the earth that we might be holy and blameless before Him; in love He predestined us to adoption through Jesus Christ unto Himself, according to the kind intention of His will, unto the praise of the glory of His

> grace which He gave to us in the Beloved. In Him we have redemption through His blood, the forgiveness of sins, according to the riches of His grace, which He lavished upon us...In whom also we were called, having been predestined according to the plan of Him who works out all things according to the intention of His will...." (Ephesians 1:3-8, 11)

The passage *seems* straightforward enough, yet many find strange and wonderful ways of getting around its teaching. So that the Word can speak for itself, let us take the text as it stands and ask a series of questions:

Q: Who blessed us with every spiritual blessing?
A: The Father.
Q: *In whom* are we blessed?
A: In Christ Jesus.
Q: What action did the Father take before the foundation of the earth?
A: He chose.
Q: Whom did He choose?
A: Us.
Q: In whom were we chosen?
A: In Christ Jesus.
Q: For what purpose were we chosen?
A: That we might be holy and blameless before Him.
Q: What action did the Father undertake in love?
A: He predestined.
Q: Whom did He predestine?
A: Us.
Q: For what purpose or goal were we predestined?
A: Unto adoption through Jesus Christ unto Himself.
Q: On what basis were we predestined?
A: According to the kind intention of His will.

Q: What is the result of His predestination in Christ?
A: The praise of His grace.
Q: What do we have in Christ Jesus?
A: Redemption, the forgiveness of sins through His blood.
Q: In whom were we called?
A: In Christ Jesus.
Q: What is the description of the text of those who are called in Him?
A: Those who were "predestined according to His plan."
Q: How does the Apostle describe the Father in verse 11?
A: As the One who "works out all things according to the intention of His will."

It was not a *mere plan* that was predestined before time, but *a people*, the very same people of whom Jesus said in John 6, "All that the Father gives me...." God's sovereign elective grace was granted to this people "before time." God's grace, then, is worthy to be praised, for the salvation of God's people is God's awesome work. He receives all the glory and honor, which could not be said if man's "cooperation" and effort were required to make the whole scheme work.

In his epistle to the Romans Paul took the opportunity to present the doctrine of salvation in a logical, thought-out style. For this reason Romans has always acted as the catalyst for reform in the Church, for anyone who seriously deals with its text is forced to abandon any man-made notions of the Gospel, and return again to the purity of God's message in Christ Jesus. If the concepts of predestination and election are part and parcel of the Gospel, then Romans will present it. And this is exactly what we find. In Romans 8:28-30 we find what has been called the "golden chain of redemption":

> "And we know that all things work together for good for those who love God, those who are called according to His purpose. For those whom He foreknew, He also predestined to be conformed to the image of His Son, that He might be the firstborn among many brethren. And those whom He predestined, these he also called; and those whom He called, these He also justified; and those whom He justified, these He also glorified."

The chain is as follows: foreknow ⇨ predestined ⇨ called ⇨ justified ⇨ glorified. There are only two consistent interpretations of this passage (as far as the passage itself is concerned): the universalist's and the Reformed. The universalist says that all men are foreknown, predestined, called, justified, and glorified. This, however, is out of harmony with the rest of the Bible's teaching, for the Scriptures speak plainly of the eternal punishment of the wicked. The Reformed interpreter says that God's elect are foreknown,[11] predestined, called, justified, and glorified. In each case the group under consideration is limited to the elect of God. The more common interpretations of modern gospel preachers, however, are inconsistent with the passage, for while most would say that those "justified and glorified" are limited in number, they would say that *all are called* (an unlimited number), and those who are foreknown and hence predestined are, in reality, determined by man's choice, not God's. But Paul's teaching is clear: God is the author and finisher of salvation; man does not figure in the above passage outside of being the *object* of God's grace. All that the Christian man does—all the good works, the striving after holiness, the seeking to glorify God—he does only because God enables him and empowers him. He does not do good works to gain or keep his salvation, but he does them because he loves the one who had mercy upon him and raised him up from death to eternal life.

Paul continues the theme of God's sovereignty into chapter 9. Little comment is required for the impact of his teaching to be felt outside of pointing out that some try to avoid the conclusions of Romans 9 by asserting that all that is under discussion here is God's election of *nations, not individual persons*. Even if this were the case, *nations are* made up of *individuals*.[12]

> "Not only that, but also Rebeccah, when she conceived by Isaac our father, before the twins were born, or had done anything good or bad, in order that the purpose of God in election might stand, not by works but by the one who calls, it was said to her that, *the greater will serve the lesser, just as it has been written, Jacob I loved, but Esau I hated*. Therefore what shall we say? There is no unrighteousness with God, is there? May it never be! For he says to Moses, *I will have mercy on whom I have mercy, and compassion on whom I have compassion*. Therefore it is not of the one willing or the one running, but God who has mercy. For the Scriptures say to Pharaoh, for this reason *I raised you up that I might demonstrate in you my power, and so that my name might be proclaimed in all the earth*. Therefore, he has mercy on whom he wishes and he hardens whom he wishes. You will say therefore to me, 'why does He still find

> fault, for who resists His will?' On the contrary, who are you, O man, who answers back to God? The thing molded will not say to the one who molded it, 'Why did you make me like this' will it? Or does not the potter have authority over the clay, out of the same lump to make indeed one vessel to honor and another unto dishonor? What if God, though willing to demonstrate his wrath and make known his power endured with much patience vessels of wrath prepared for destruction, also in order that He might make known the riches of His glory upon vessels of mercy which he foreordained unto glory, even us whom also he called...."

God's mercy and compassion, then, cannot be *demanded* by anyone. Not one person deserves God's grace, so no charge of "unfairness" can be lodged when someone gets what they deserve rather than mercy and grace. Paul asserts that *"it is not of the one willing or the one running, but God who has mercy."* A succinct summary of the sovereignty of God in salvation indeed! Man is not the decision maker, man is not the deciding factor. God wills, God accomplishes. It is God's work.

Yet, man must immediately respond in rebellion: the imaginary objector quickly asserts that if salvation is utterly God's work, then God must be unrighteous! How many today lodge the same objection against the teaching of God's electing grace! But Paul's answer is quick: *"Who are you, O man, who answers back to God?"* Is this really an answer? Most would not be satisfied with it. Yet, it says volumes if we listen carefully. His response is based upon the whole Biblical concept of God as Creator being utterly free do with His creation as He sees fit. The audacity of sinful man to stand up and shake his fist in God's face and say, "You are unfair! I deserve better!" But Paul reminds man of his created nature, his finitude. God is not unjust, and man is not God's judge so as to be able to charge Him with unrighteousness.

So we see that God elects to save on the basis of His own will and purpose, and nothing else. But how does God save? What method has He chosen? How is the work of Jesus Christ related to our salvation? What is redemption, reconciliation, and justification? What is forgiveness of sins, and what is its extent? To these topics we now turn.

Chapter 6
The Atonement of the Lord Jesus Christ

The central aspect of the Biblical doctrine of salvation is the work of Jesus Christ. Few, no matter what their beliefs, would dispute that statement. Yet, His work is understood in a myriad of differing ways. We have seen the concept of the Mass and the *"re-presentation"* of the death of Christ at Calvary that it supposedly contains. Many view the work of Christ as simply "removing legal bars" so that man can make the final decision to follow Christ or not. Others see the death of Christ simply as *the great example*, to be followed and imitated by everyone today, yet in itself it is not really relevant to sin or its forgiveness.

With all these different voices crying for our attention, how are we to really understand the work of Christ? How can we know with any certainty the reason of His death, and the effect thereof? Thankfully, we have the inspired Scriptures to guide us, to reveal to us God's intention in sending Jesus Christ, and the effect of His death. Few topics in the Bible are more often addressed than the atoning work of Jesus Christ, and this *includes the Old Testament*, where the sacrificial laws prefigured the work of Christ, and the prophets such as Isaiah looked forward to His death (Isaiah 53).

To understand the atonement of Christ, we must first build a proper foundation from the Word of God. Therefore, we will begin with definitions, something that is all too often ignored in a discussion such as this. We will define terms like *atonement, propitiation, reconciliation, redemption, and justification*. These terms will be defined *in light of the original languages of the text and their specific usage in the Bible itself*. Next, the *intention* of Christ's coming will be examined. Does the Bible tell us exactly *why Christ came*? Why is it important to understand this? Did He accomplish His intended design? Then we will look at Christ's function as our High Priest, focusing primarily on the relationship between Christ's sacrifice on the cross and His work of intercession. Then we shall ask, "for whom was the atonement made?" What is the extent of the atonement of Christ? In answering this question we will consider the nature of faith and repentance, and see that these two are the gifts of God, not the natural abilities of fallen man. Then we shall ask,"what is the effect of the atonement?" The Roman Catholic teachings will be seen to be utterly incompatible with the Biblical presentation of the work of Christ. Specific Scripture passages utilized by Romanism in defense of its teachings will be examined in the following chapter.

Definitions

No meaningful communication can take place without definitions. Both parties in a conversation must have the same definitions of terms or chaos will result. So, too, when we come to the pages of Scripture, we must allow the Bible to define its own terms, rather than importing our own meanings so as to come out with the teaching we were intending to find in the first place. If we allow the Scriptures to speak for themselves, we will find a consistent, harmonious truth presented throughout, for the Scriptures partake of the wholeness and symmetry of their Author.

The doctrine of the atonement utilizes a group of special words which, together, express various of the facets of this central aspect of Christian faith. The first of these terms to be examined is the term "atonement."

Atonement refers to the covering of sins. The Hebrew term *kaphar* is related to an Arabic root meaning "to cover, conceal." There may be an illusion to the meaning of *kaphar* in the sprinkling of the mercy seat with the blood of the sacrifice on *yom kippur*, the Day of Atonement. When a sin was *atoned* for, it was forgiven. In the instructions relating to the Day of Atonement in Leviticus 16, a goat was to be sent into the wilderness after having hands laid upon its head "to make atonement upon it" (Leviticus 16:10, 21). It is said that all the iniquities and transgressions of the people would be placed upon the "scapegoat" and sent away from the people. This makes clear that "atonement" then does not simply mean "covering" but *"forgiving"*. The sacrifice of atonement satisfies God and brings forgiveness of the sin. As the Psalmist could say, "As far as the east is from the west, so far has He removed our transgressions from us" (Psalm 103:12). Hence, to simply take the word to mean "cover" without also understanding the *removal* of sin would be a mistake. Nothing, of course, can be "covered" from the sight of God; so, if sins are said to be "covered" then they are dealt with in God's eyes. It must also be emphasized that *when a sin is atoned for and forgiven, no "punishment" remains to be "expiated."* **All of sin** is removed in atonement—its guilt *and its punishment*.

The actual term "atonement" is not used in the New Testament.[1] Why, then, should it be used of the "atonement of Christ" when it is not used in the one place where this work is most clearly explained? The term functions to explain in a general way the many faceted presentation of the death of Christ. More *specific* terms are used in the New Testament, but all together are accurately described as "atonement" as it is found in the Law, and we will use it to describe the work of Christ as a general term.

Propitiation

A group of terms together express the meaning of "propitiation" in the New Testament. The first, *hilasmos* (ἱλασμός), refers to that which *expiates and propitiates sin*. But what do these terms mean? Expiation refers to a "removal of guilt," "satisfaction" or "making atonement." All of these thoughts are found in the Greek term *hilasmos*. Sin's guilt is removed in expiation, and satisfaction is made for the punishment of sin as well. But this is not *all* that the term refers to. To stop only *with expiation* is to miss the meaning of the term. Yes, sin is forgiven, guilt removed by expiation. But *hilasmos* also refers to the *removal of the anger and wrath of God*, hence the more proper translation of "propitiation." *When propitiation is made for sin, not only is the guilt of sin removed, but the wrath of God against that sin and that sinner is removed (satisfied) as well.* This is **very important** for the Roman Catholic to understand, for if sin is propitiated in the New Testament sense, the wrath of God, *including the punishment due to sin*, is satisfied and done away with. Why is punishment satisfied as well? Because when sin is propitiated, *there no longer remains any ground for punishment!* The punishment due the sin has been laid upon the sacrificial victim, and hence the penalty is fulfilled! The person whose sin is propitiated is then *right with God*, for what had alienated from God is now removed by sacrifice.

Some of the other terms include *hilaskomai* (ἱλάσκομαι) meaning "to make propitiation" and *hilasterion* (ἱλαστήριον), that which propitiates. The last term is used in the Greek translation of the Old Testament (the Septuagint) to describe the mercy seat, upon which the blood of the sacrifice was sprinkled, showing how closely the term "atonement" is connected with "propitiation."

Jesus is the propitiation for sin according to Scripture. Paul taught, "...being justified freely by His grace through the redemption which is in Christ Jesus, whom God foreordained as the propitiation through faith in His blood..." (Romans 3:25). The blood of Christ is set forth as the grounds of the propitiation. Redemption and justification are closely connected with the propitiation of sin in Christ Jesus; indeed, as we shall see, redemption and justification flow directly from the atoning work of Christ, in fact, *all for whom the atonement is made are thereby redeemed and justified.*[2] Note as well that *there is no other means of propitiation for sin.*[3] Jesus Christ is the only way in which sin can be forgiven, remitted, satisfied.

Hebrews 2:17 says, "Therefore He had to be made like the brethren in all things, in order that He might become a merciful and faithful high priest in things pertaining to God, to make *propitiation* for the sins of the people." Here the writer of Hebrews teaches that Jesus' role as high priest was so that He might make propitiation for the sins of the people. This means that Christ's death has atoned for sin. *There can be no other propitiation if Christ has already atoned for sin.* Sin is either propitiated or it is not. Sin is not "partially propitiated." It is either forgiven, removed, or it is not. If Christ functions as the High Priest and is the propitiation for a person's sins, then those sins are completely and fully removed.

John wrote, "And if anyone sins, we have an Advocate with the Father, Jesus Christ the righteous; and He Himself is the propitiation for our sins, not for ours only, but for the sins of the whole world."[4] Jesus Christ is **the** propitiation for sins—there is no other. In love the Father sent the Son *to be the propitiation* for our sins (1 John 4:10). Here is an infinite person who must then in His death make an infinite propitiation for sin.

Reconciliation

Reconciliation speaks of the mending of a broken relationship. In the New Testament, the term is never used with God as its object; that is, it is not said that "God is reconciled to man." God is the one who initiates reconciliation. It is His initiative that brings about reconciliation through the death of Jesus Christ. Yet, there is a sense in which it is proper to speak of God being "reconciled" to man, as long as that is not taken in such a way as to construe God as having done wrong, resulting in the rupture of the original relationship between Himself and man. God partakes of the *fruit* of the reconciliation wrought in the death of Christ.

> "But God demonstrates His own love to us in that while we were yet sinners Christ died in our behalf. Much more then, having now been justified in His blood, we shall be saved by Him from the (coming) wrath. For if, while we were enemies, we were reconciled to God through the death of His Son, how much more having been reconciled shall we be saved through His life. And not only this but we also rejoice in God through our Lord Jesus Christ, through whom we have now received the reconciliation."

The inter-play of the group of terms we are studying is striking in this passage. Paul asserts that Christ died in our behalf, even while we were sinners, alienated from God. He then asserts that this means that we have been justified (made righteous) in His blood, showing clearly that for Paul justification is the natural result of being the object of the atoning work of Christ—if Christ dies for you, the ground of your justification is laid by that action. There is no other basis upon which justification can be maintained than if all impedances (sins, impurities) to that state of righteousness are removed; and the only way any sinner can have his sins removed is in the blood of Jesus Christ. The one who is justified in the blood of Christ is then safe from the wrath of God. Why? If one is washed in the blood of Christ, then there remains no basis for God's wrath to come against a person. *This is extremely important to remember with reference to the Roman concept of sin, for in Romanism it is taught that one can be forgiven of sin, and yet still suffer the wrath of God in temporal punishments*. Paul then goes on to assert that the condition of *enmity* that existed between sinners and God is removed through the death of Christ. We are reconciled to God through the work of Christ, for in that work Christ removed all barriers to fellowship by taking the sins of His people upon Himself. Could it truly be said that reconciliation has taken place when one of the two parties (the reconciled sinner) has still to undergo punishment and make satisfaction for his sins? Note that in the text the reconciliation is *past-tense*—it is a finished action. We *have been reconciled*, and because we have, we will be saved through His life. That is, just as Paul had explained earlier (4:25), Christ was delivered up for our transgressions, and He was raised for our justification. His death clears away the debt of sin, and His resurrection (His life) provides for our right standing with God. Finally, this reconciliation is *only and solely* ours through Jesus Christ. Paul says that we rejoice or exult in God, "through whom we have now received the reconciliation." *There simply is no way to receive reconciliation with God through any means other than Jesus Christ, and that specifically in His finished work of atonement.* Reconciliation flows from the cross of Calvary, and nowhere else.

The same themes are struck by Paul in Colossians 1:21-22, where he writes, "And though you were once alienated and hostile in mind, [busy] in evil deeds, yet He has now reconciled you in His fleshly body through death, in order that He might present you holy and blameless before Him...." Reconciliation takes place because of the death of Christ. The result of being reconciled to God through the death of Christ is that we might be "holy and blameless before Him." Holiness and blamelessness demand the purity of the individual, and this is the effect of the death of Jesus Christ.

Finally, in 1 Corinthians 5:18-20 we have a further elaboration of the meaning of reconciliation. Specifically, in verse 19 we read that God was, by Christ, reconciling the world to Himself. What is the content of this reconciliation? How is it that the world is reconciled to God in Christ? Paul explains the meaning of reconciliation as, "not counting (or reckoning) their trespasses against them." We shall take leave to discuss the extent of the term "world" at a later point; for now the emphasis in our study is upon the *meaning* of the term "reconciliation," and here it is defined in part as "not counting their trespasses against them." How can a holy God not reckon the penalty of sin upon those who are sinners? Christ has borne their sin, *and their penalty*, upon Himself. Their sin *and its penalty* was laid upon Christ as their substitute, hence God can look at them as righteous because they truly are righteous, their sins having been atoned for and removed.

At this point it is important to emphasize the *substitutionary* aspect of the Lord's atonement. Christ died as the substitute for sinful man. He bore *all the penalty* that was due to sin, in that He became sin in our place. Paul taught, "He made Him who knew no sin to be sin in our place, so that we might become the righteousness of God in Him" (2 Corinthians 5:21). Christ became sin in our place, and in so doing removed sin—all of sin, every bit of sin—from God's people. The result of this is that those who are in Christ Jesus are made the righteousness of God. This is the only condition in which one can stand before God, clothed in His righteousness. No amount of suffering, no amount of purging, can ever cause one to have the righteousness of God. All you have when you clean up a sinful man is a man standing in human righteousness. When Christ dies in behalf of a man, as His substitute, that man receives the righteousness of God in Christ, and is by this made fit to stand before the Holy One of Israel. Christ's position as the *substitute for God's people* guarantees the effectiveness of His atoning work. Why? Christ is the **perfect** substitute. He is able to bear *all the sins and iniquities* of God's people, and in so doing, takes those sins away—completely. As a substitute, Christ bears all the guilt *and punishment* of sin for the one for whom He substitutes. The *vicarious* nature of the atonement is clearly prophesied in Isaiah's vision of the Suffering Servant, Isaiah 53:

> "Surely our griefs He Himself bore,
> And our sorrows He carried...
> But He was pierced through for our transgressions,
> He was crushed for our iniquities;

> The chastening for our well-being fell upon
> Him,
> And by His scourging we are healed.
> All of us like sheep have gone astray,
> Each of us has turned to his own way;
> But the LORD has caused the iniquity of
> us all
> To fall on Him...
> But the LORD was pleased
> To crush Him, putting Him to grief;
> If He would render Himself as a guilt
> offering,
> He will see His offspring,
> He will prolong His days,
> And the good pleasure of the LORD will
> prosper in His hand....
> By His knowledge the Righteous One,
> My Servant, will justify the many,
> As He will bear their iniquities."
> (Isaiah 53:4,5,6,10,11, NASB)

Here is the Perfect Substitute, the One who takes the sins, iniquities, and punishments of God's people upon Himself, and in so doing, He "justifies the many" by bearing their iniquities. If Christ, then, has died as the substitute for His people, then they are, by virtue of His death alone, released from the bondage of sin. His is not a *hypothetical* substitution, but a *real one*.

The concept of the vicarious atonement of Christ, though professed by many today in the "fundamentalist" movement, is often denied in practice. In reality, those who do not hold to the doctrine of the *specific or definite atonement* of Christ, that being the truth that Christ died as the substitute for the elect of God *only*, do not really hold to a *real substitutionary atonement*. When asked if Christ died in the place of any single man so as to secure his salvation, the modern evangelical will frequently respond, "well, Christ died for every man so as to *make salvation possible*." But that is not the question. Did He die as the substitute for every man, and in so doing secure salvation *without reference to any contingent human action*? Most will not say this, for they do not believe that all will be saved. The Reformed faith asserts that Christ's death, without being dependent upon any human actions, is not only *sufficient* to save, but that it actually *does save*. Any other position makes the effectiveness of Christ's death contingent upon the actions of men. Right here the similarity between the Roman Catholic position and the non-Reformed position of so much of modern American evangelicalism can be seen, for Romanism teaches that the effects of Christ's sacrifice in the Mass (the degree of the forgiveness of temporal punishments) are dependent upon man's actions, both in his communication at Mass and his disposition in so doing. Many Evangelicals, while not accepting the Roman concept, also believe that the death of Christ is of no effect for a large number of those for whom it was supposedly made, for those people do not "make it effective for themselves" by believing. In both cases, the atonement of Christ remains *hypothetical and ineffective* until the actions or will of man comes into play to *finish the work*! We shall have more to say about this below when we discuss the extent of the atoning work of Christ, but for now it is important to note that if Christ dies substitutionarily for a person, that person cannot fail but receive the benefit of that death in the forgiveness of his sins.

Redemption

The Greek term[5] translated in the New Testament as "redemption" was used in secular literature to describe the freeing of a slave through the payment of a ransom.

The slave was freed from his bondage by this transaction. So, too, in the New Testament redemption refers to the freeing of the sinner from the bondage of sin because of the atoning work of Christ. The death of Christ is seen as *payment in full*, resulting in freedom from condemnation for those who are in Christ. This redemption is "in Christ Jesus" as Paul said in Romans 3:24: "...being justified freely by His grace through the redemption which is in Christ Jesus." The righteous position which is the believer's by the grace of God is made possible because of this "redemption which is in Christ Jesus." This redemption is described by Paul in Colossians 1:14 as "the forgiveness of sins." It is the power of sin that enslaves, and hence, when the power of sin is broken by the death of Christ, those once held captive are set free.

Some Roman Catholics believe that redemption is simply the "removal of legal bars" that stand in man's way. These would assert that Christ did indeed redeem all men, but that this simply makes it possible for them to then come to God for salvation. But this is to misunderstand the Bible's teaching. Redemption is the forgiveness of sins, not simply in a theoretical manner, but in reality. We can be righteous in God's sight (justified) because the sin problem has been eradicated in Christ's death. If Christ, then, died for all men, then all men are redeemed, and their sins are forgiven. On what basis could they then be condemned or punished? What grounds would God have for His wrath against sin? He would have none, and hence all would be saved.[6]

The Intention of Christ's Work

With these definitions in mind, let us now turn to this question: What was the intention of Christ's coming into this world? Why did Christ enter into human flesh and dwell among His own creatures? This is no frivolous question, for once we determine the answer, we must ask a further question: Did He accomplish the ends for which He came?

The answer to the first question seems to be agreeable to most parties who venture an answer. As Jesus Himself said, "For the Son of Man came to seek *and to save* the lost" (Luke 19:10). Here is the answer from His own lips. He came to seek and to save the lost. This is echoed by His Apostle's words to Timothy, "This is a faithful saying and worthy of all acceptance: Christ Jesus came into the world to save sinners, of whom I am the first" (I Timothy 1:15). Paul believes the same as Jesus. Christ's intention in coming into the world is *to save sinners, those who are "lost."*

Such seems so plain as to be unarguable. And yet, the second question does not receive as unanimous an answer as the first. When it is asked whether Christ achieved His intended goal, many different responses are offered, if indeed the question is considered at all. But it is important to press the matter. *Did* Christ accomplish His goal? Did He save sinners? The question is not, "did He make the salvation of sinners *possible*" but "did He *actually* save sinners by His death?" This is not simply a matter of theological subtlety, it is a question that strikes at the very heart of the Gospel itself, for it inquires into the effect of the death of Christ. It may be expressed like this: *Is the death of Christ, without any additional work, complete and perfect, fully able to save man and bring him to glory*? Is the work of Christ incomplete without man's faith or works? Is it necessary for one to go through sacraments or ceremonies to complete the work *begun* on the cross? It is our contention that the death of Christ is complete in and of itself, and does not need man's faith or his participation in sacraments or ceremonies to attain perfection. There simply is no way for anyone to hold to the teaching of the New Testament and assert that the death of Christ is only hypothetical outside of human initiative and action. Christ's death is a perfect and completed work performed by the Perfect Substitute. His death, then, is *powerful to save* simply because it is the work of God and is *not dependent upon man.*

We freely admit that this doctrine, that of the *definite atonement of Christ,* is not popular today. Surely the Roman Catholic position is in disagreement, as we have already seen from a review of the doctrine of the Mass. *If Christ's death actually saves those for whom it is made, then obviously the Mass is in contradiction to the work of Christ for there would be no need of a "re-presentation" of His death since those for whom the atonement is made are perfected thereby.* While Romanism continuously asserts that the sacrifice of the Mass and the sacrifice of the cross are one and the same, if the Bible teaches the definite and finished atonement of Christ, then the Roman claim is shown to be false, and the Roman system in error.

But it is not only the Roman teaching that is challenged by the assertion of the definite atonement of Christ. The majority of popular presentations of the Gospel neglect, out of fear of offending people, to assert the work of Christ as it is presented in Scripture, for to do so would be to imply that salvation is totally and completely the work of God, and this is hardly how one makes loads of "converts." Holding to the Gospel message as it is found in Scripture demands the work of God to bring a person to repentance. If you hold to a "universal atonement" (that is, if you believe Christ died for all men indiscriminately, and that His death does not actually save, but only makes salvation possible), read on. Look to the Word of God and accept only its authority. It is our opinion that the non-Reformed position can say nothing to Romanism in regards to the work of Christ, for it compromises on the very central issue of the atonement.

Christ's Intercessory Work

Before looking specifically at the *extent* of the atonement (whether limited or universal), it is important to understand the relationship between the *atonement* of Christ and His *intercessory* work. We shall also see that there is a close relationship between the work of Christ as *Priest* and the work of Christ as *Intercessor*. In fact, we will see that the former is the basis of, and the substance of, the latter.

The intercessory work of Christ is explicitly discussed in Hebrews 7:24-25:

> "But He, on the other hand, because He abides forever, holds His priesthood unchangeably, hence, He is also able to save completely those who come unto God by Him, as He lives forever to make intercession on their behalf."

Here the writer of Hebrews asserts that Christ *is able* to save "to the uttermost" those who come unto God through Him. And why does Christ have this ability? Because of His ministry of intercession before the Father. But we have alleged above that it is the *death* of Christ that saves, not any further works after this. Is this a contradiction? Only if the intercession of Christ is an action or operation that is distinct from His death. But it is just here that we need to recognize that the work of Christ as intercessor is not *disconnected* from His work as Priest in the offering of Himself. Paul brought out the "priestly" aspect of Christ's work clearly in

Ephesians 5:2:

> "...and walk in love, just as also Christ loved us and delivered Himself up in our behalf, an offering and a sacrifice to God as a fragrant aroma."

The terms "offering" and "sacrifice" come straight from the Levitical concepts of sacrifice in the law. The writer of Hebrews also used this kind of language in describing the work of Christ:

> "But when Christ appeared as high priest of the good things to come, (He entered) through the greater and more perfect tabernacle not made by hands, that is, not of this creation, neither did he enter the holy place once for all through the blood of goats and calves, but through His own blood, having obtained eternal redemption." (Hebrews 9:11-12)

On what basis does Christ enter into the Holy Place? Not through the blood of goats and calves, but through His own blood. He enters into the presence of the Father, *having obtained eternal redemption*. Christ presents Himself before the Father as the perfect oblation in behalf of His people. His work of intercession, then, is based on His work of atonement. Intercession is not *another or different kind* of work, but is the *presentation* of the work of the cross before the Father.[7] Jesus does not implore the Father to be merciful to men without grounds for that mercy, does He? Would the Son ask the Father to compromise His holiness and justice by simply overlooking sin? Surely not! Rather, the Son intercedes for men before the Father on the basis of the fact that in His death He has taken away the sins of God's people, and therefore, by presenting His finished work on Calvary before the Father, He assures the application of the benefits of His death to those for whom He intercedes. Note as well that the *extent* of the intercessory work of Christ *is identical to the extent* of the atonement of Christ; that is, Christ intercedes for the same people for whom He died. Christ does not intercede for people for whom He did not die, for He would have no basis upon which to intercede; nor does He not intercede for anyone for whom He died, for this would involve an inconsistency in Christ. All those for whom Christ died will be the objects of His intercession. And, since we know that none for whom the Son intercedes will ever be lost (for if this could happen, then there would be a contradiction in the Godhead, the Son willing to save someone, the Father refusing), it is demonstrated again that all for whom Christ died will be brought into their salvation.

It might be asserted in reply that Christ intercedes for *all men*. Does not 1 Timothy 2:5 say, "For there is one God, and one mediator between God and men, the man Christ Jesus"? Does this not indicate that Christ is mediator for all men, and hence must intercede for them? The great Puritan writer John Owen replied,

> "What then, I pray? what will be concluded hence? Cannot Christ be a mediator between God and men, but he must be a mediator for all men? Are not the elect men? do not the children partake of flesh and blood? doth not his church consist of men? What reason is there to assert, out of an indefinite proposition, a universal conclusion? Because Christ was a mediator for men (which were true had he been

> so only for his apostles), shall we conclude therefore he was so for all men?"[8]

Indeed, it should be noted that when the Lord Jesus prayed to the Father in John 17 (what is commonly known as His "High Priestly Prayer"), He specifically indicated that His intercession at that point was **not** for the "whole world." He prayed for His disciples and those who would believe on Him through their word, but in verse 9 He prays, "I am not asking concerning the world, but those You gave Me..."

The Extent of the Atonement

So we address the question, *"for whom did Christ die?"* The Reformed answer has already been given above: Christ died substitutionarily for the elect. His death provides full and perfect salvation for them. But is this what the Bible says? We will review a number of passages to discover whether the Reformed position is solidly based in Scripture.

The Lord Jesus said, "The Son of Man did not come to be served, but to serve, and to give His life a ransom for many" (Matthew 20:28). The Lord seems to be borrowing here from the prophecy of Isaiah where it is said that God's Righteous Servant will "justify the many." It is not claimed that the term "many" *proves* a limitation in the atonement; but it is strange that *if the atonement is universal in scope*, that a limited term would be used. And, when the rest of the testimony of Scripture is allowed to speak as well, the choice of words by our Lord will become significant.

When speaking of the laying down of His life in John 10, Jesus was very specific in regards to *who* was the beneficiary of His death. We read in John 10:11, 15:

> "I am the good Shepherd. The good

> Shepherd lays down His life in behalf of the sheep...just as the Father knows Me and I know the Father, and I lay down My life in behalf of the sheep."

Jesus claims that He lays down His life in behalf of the sheep. Who are the sheep? The sheep are those who are given to the Son by the Father (10:29; cf. 6:37),[9] who are known by the Son, and who know the Son's voice, and follow Him (10:14, 27). It is to the sheep that He gives eternal life (10:28). Obviously, all who do not receive eternal life are, therefore, not of Christ's sheep. Jesus explicitly informed the Jews who did not believe in Him, "you do not believe because you are not of My sheep" (10:26). These Jews were not of His sheep, and, therefore, He did not lay down His life for them.

Jesus also indicated that the greatest expression of love was for a man to lay down his life for his friends (John 15:13). He then indicated that His disciples were His friends. Can it be said that those who do not receive eternal life are Christ's friends? Is this not a limited group, especially in light of the fact that Jesus speaks of these His disciples as a *distinct group* from the rest of the world in John 17? This seems surely to be the case. The angel who announced the birth of Christ to Joseph in Matthew 1:21 seemed to be sure of who would benefit from the work of Christ as well, for he said, "And she will bear a Son, and you will call His name Jesus, *for He will save His people from their sins*." Christ will certainly save *His people from their sins*. He will not simply **try to save** His people, but He **will** save His people. This is the promise of the Word of God.

The *definite atonement* of Christ is presented with clarity in the epistles of Paul. In Ephesians 5 we read,

> "And walk in love, just as Christ *loved us*

> *and gave Himself up in our behalf,* an offering and a sacrifice to God as a fragrant aroma...Husbands, love your wives, just as Christ loved the Church and delivered Himself up *in her behalf,* in order that He might sanctify her, having cleansed her by the washing of water with the word, in order that He might present to Himself the church in all her glory, having no spot or wrinkle or any such thing; but that she should be holy and blameless."

Paul teaches that Christ laid down His life *in behalf of the Church,* so that He might present her holy and blameless before Him. The Church corporately partakes of what happens to the individual in Ephesians 1:4; that is, the Church is holy and blameless just as the individual member of her is holy and blameless in Jesus Christ. The purification of the Church is said to be the purpose for which Christ delivered Himself up in her behalf. Can we doubt, then, that the purpose for which Christ died will then be accomplished? And if Christ's death *surely* results in the spotlessness and purity of the Church for whom He died, how can it be said that Christ died for millions and millions who shall die impure and never partake of the benefits of His death?

It has been said that if the epistle to the Romans is the cathedral of the New Testament, the eighth chapter is the pinnacle, the spire. In this great passage of Scripture, Paul begins by asserting that there is no condemnation for those who are in Christ Jesus (*contra* the Council of Trent's idea of someone dying "in Christ yet not fully purified"). The chapter speaks of those who are "according to the Spirit" and the adoption as sons of God that is theirs. Then, like a Beethoven symphony building to a climax, Paul launches into the great description of the salvation of God's elect, being foreknown, predestined, called, justified, and glorified (8:29-30). Following right on the heels of this we read,

> "What shall we say to these things? If God is for us, who can be against us? He who did not spare His own Son, but delivered Him up *for us all*, will He not also with Him freely give us all things? Who shall bring a charge against the elect of God? God is the one justifying. Who is the one condemning? Christ Jesus who died, yes, rather, who was raised, who is at the right hand of the God, who also *intercedes* for us" (Romans 8:31-34).

For whom was Christ delivered up? For "us all." Who is this? Immediately Paul identifies them: the elect of God. Note again the intimate connection made here between the death of Christ and His office of intercession. And who is the specific object of His intercession? Again, the elect of God. What an incredible position of grace is the inheritance of the elect of God! They are redeemed by Christ, who also continues to intercede for them before the Father. Who can bring a charge against God's elect indeed! What charge could possibly "stick" when God is the one who judges His people "righteous" and the Lord Jesus Christ, the Son of God, has died in their place and ever lives to make intercession for them! No grounds for condemnation exist for those for whom Christ has died.

The confession of the Church can be seen in Paul's letter to Titus:

> "We are looking for the blessed hope and the appearing of the glory of our great God and Savior, the Lord Jesus Christ,

> who gave Himself *for us*, that He might redeem us from every lawless deed, and purify for Himself a people for His own possession, zealous for good deeds" (Titus 2:13-14)

The Christian Church confesses that Christ gave Himself *for us*, in thankful recognition of our redemption that is in Him. Christ died so as to "purify for Himself a people for His own possession." Shall He accomplish His intended goal? The heart stirred by the Holy Spirit answers "yes!" Indeed, on the personal level, the Christian is almost over-awed when faced with the truth of Paul's words in Galatians 2:20:

> "I have been crucified with Christ, and I no longer live, but Christ lives in me. And the life I now live in the flesh, I live by the faith of the Son of God who loved me and delivered Himself up in my behalf."

The Christian has been crucified with Christ, in that, as Paul taught, we were united with Christ before the creation of the world (Ephesians 1:4) so that His death becomes our death, His resurrection our resurrection. We died with Christ, and Christ now lives His life in us. He who loved us and delivered Himself up in our behalf lives His life through us, empowering us, guiding us by His Holy Spirit.

So we see the testimony of the Scriptures that Christ died for a specific people: He died for "many," for "His sheep," for "the Church," for "the elect of God," for "His friends," for "us" and for "me."

The Gifts of Repentance and Faith

Yet, many oppose this teaching, saying that it limits

the effectiveness of the work of Christ. Yet, just the opposite is true. The Reformed understanding limits the *intention* of Christ's work, but asserts that it is *fully capable of accomplishing its goal.* The non-Reformed view, however, limits the *effect* of the atonement by making it dependent upon man's actions. The most popular presentation of this view is that Christ died for all, but man must accept His death for it to become effective. That is, man must add *faith* to the work of Christ. But is this Biblical?

No one will argue that the Bible calls men to repent and believe in Christ Jesus. The question can best be understood in asking whether man, outside of the supernatural work of God, is *able to believe* in Christ. We saw above that Jesus taught that man in sin is *incapable* of coming to Him outside of the drawing of the Father (John 6:44, 65). Beyond this, the truth is that *both repentance and faith are the gifts of God.* Man is not capable of repenting or believing outside of the supernatural enablement of God. Let us look to Scripture to find this teaching.

In both Romans 2:4 and 2 Timothy 2:24-25, Paul uses language that suggests to us that repentance is the work of God in man. In Romans 2:4 we read, "Or do you despise the riches of His kindness and patience toward you, not knowing that God's kindness leads you to repentance?" And in writing to Timothy, Paul discussed those who opposed the teaching of sound doctrine, telling Timothy to instruct such people with patience, "if perhaps God may grant them repentance unto a real knowledge of the truth." God is pictured as *granting* repentance to man. If it must be granted by God, is it the natural ability of man?

Furthermore, when Peter replied to the authorities who instructed him not to preach in the name of Jesus any longer, he replied that it was better to obey God than men, and, in bearing testimony to Christ, said, "this one God exalted to His right hand as Prince and Savior, to give repentance unto Israel, and forgiveness of sins." Christ is described as giving or granting to Israel repentance, as well as forgiveness of sins. Few would argue that forgiveness of sins is the gift of God; hence, repentance is the gift of God as well.

But the most striking passage on the fact that repentance *must* be the gift of God is found in Paul's discussion of the "natural mind" in Romans 8. Here we find a description of the differences between the "mind set on the flesh" and the "mind set on the Spirit." The mind set on the flesh is death, the Apostle teaches, and the mind set on the Spirit is life and peace. Then a description of the "fleshly mind" is provided. We must seriously consider what is said by Paul. It is far too easy in our humanistic age to dismiss as irrelevant his insight into human nature outside of God's grace. But for the person who accepts the inspiration and authority of Scripture, passages such as this give us information about man that is true and factual. We simply will not have a proper view of humankind if we ignore what the Word teaches about man in his sin. Paul said,

> "Because the fleshly mind is hostile toward God, for it does not subject itself to the law of God, *neither is it able to do so*, and the ones who are fleshly are *unable to please God*" (Romans 8:7-8).

The natural man, one who is unregenerate, is hostile toward God. He is the enemy of God. The fleshly mind does not subject itself to the law of God, for it continues to maintain its sinful rebellion and denial of the proper place of God as Creator, itself as the creation. In fact, Paul asserts, *the natural mind is incapable of subjecting itself to the law of God.* All systems of religious belief that are built upon a view of man that presents him as **capable** of initiating his own salvation, coming to God outside of spiritual regeneration, etc., is anti-Biblical for it ignores this clear teaching of Scripture. Furthermore, Paul asserts that anyone outside of Christ, that is, anyone still in the "flesh" rather than the Spirit, is simply incapable of pleasing God. No level of human morality, no amount of good works, can possibly please God as long as a person remains in the state of spiritual death.

Since this is so, we must ask the question, is repentance pleasing to God? Such a question seems absurd, for the answer is so obvious and plain. Repentance is pleasing to God. Since this is so, then can the person who is "fleshly," who has not yet been born again, but remains in the natural condition of man outside of God's grace, repent? The answer is just as obvious: no, he cannot. Repentance, then, must be the gift of God, given to the regenerate man, as was seen in the above Scriptures.

And what of faith? We could apply the above passage to faith as well, for surely faith is pleasing to God just as repentance is. But the Scriptures are even more plain in teaching that faith is a supernatural action, and the gift of God Himself. Paul confessed that "the grace of our Lord was poured out on me abundantly, along with the faith and love that are in Christ Jesus" (I Timothy 1:14). Surely grace is a supernatural gift; love of God is a supernatural gift; therefore, faith, too, is a supernatural gift. Paul listed "faith"[10] as one of those operations of the Spirit of God in the Christian's life in Galatians 5:22. If love, joy, peace, patience, etc. are the works of the Spirit of God, faith is no less so.

It is recognized that the result of accepting faith as the work of God is to understand that regeneration,

God's action of bringing a spiritually dead person to life, must *precede* faith and repentance, as these are gifts that are given only to the saved person. A *common* belief of many is that man's faith and repentance *results in regeneration*. But we see by an examination of Scripture that this is not so. God's work *precedes* any action on the part of man. This is not to say that man does not repent, does not believe, etc., but that man is *unable* to do these things outside of the *enabling* action of God *which is always effective in bringing about what God intends*.

The Apostle John also believed that regeneration precedes faith. In I John 5:1 he wrote, "Everyone believing that Jesus is the Christ has been born from God." An examination of the Greek text reveals that all those who are born of God believe; that is, being born of God *precedes* believing.[11] First one is born from God, then one believes in Christ.

Finally, Paul asserted that it is "by grace you have been saved through faith, and that not of yourselves, it is the gift of God, not of works, lest any man should boast." When Paul says, "and that not of yourselves" his words do not refer only to the "faith" mentioned before, but to the whole preceding phrase, including grace, salvation, **and faith**.

Therefore, since both faith and repentance are the gifts of God, they will surely be given to all those for whom Christ died, for as Paul said, "He who did not spare His own Son, but delivered Him up *for us all*, will He not also with Him freely give us all things?" And what of the concept that Christ died for all, but His death is only made effective by man's faith? Such is seen to be untenable, for would Christ die for those to whom the Father has not willed to give faith? Surely not. All those for whom Christ died will also receive saving faith as the efficacious gift of the Father (Romans 8:32).

A century ago the great Baptist preacher Charles Haddon Spurgeon addressed the difference between the doctrine of the atonement as taught in Scripture, and that presented by the non-Reformed, or "Arminian" position, which, at this point, is in agreement with the Roman perspective in that it posits a universal, or non-definite atonement. In a sermon entitled "Particular Redemption" he said,

> "We are often told that we limit the atonement of Christ, because we say that Christ has not made a satisfaction for all men, or all men would be saved. Now, our reply to this is, that, on the other hand, our opponents limit it, we do not. The Arminian says, 'Christ died for all men.' Ask them what they mean by it. Did Christ die so as to secure the salvation of all men? They say, 'No, certainly not.' We ask them the next question—Did Christ die so as to secure the salvation of any man in particular? They answer, 'No.' They are obliged to admit this, if they are consistent. They say 'No; Christ has died that any man may be saved if'—and then follow certain conditions of salvation. We say, then, we will just go back to the old statement—Christ did not die so as beyond a doubt to secure the salvation of anybody, did he? You must say, 'No'; you are obliged to say so, for you believe that even after a man has been pardoned, he may yet fall from grace, and perish. Now, who is it that limits the death of Christ? Why, you. You say that Christ did not die so as to infallibly secure the salvation of

> anybody. We beg your pardon, when you say we limit Christ's death; we say, 'No, my dear sir, it is you that do it.' We say Christ so died that he infallibly secured the salvation of a multitude that no man can number, who through Christ's death not only may be saved, but are saved, must be saved, and cannot by any possibility run the hazard of being anything but saved. You are welcome to your atonement; you may keep it. We will never renounce ours for the sake of it."[12]

The great Baptist preacher would be shocked, I believe, to see how few of those who call themselves "Baptist" today agree with his views. But the Word of God does not change even though men's ideas do. The atonement is just as effective and powerful today as it was then, and the truth of the definite and saving atonement of Christ is just as important for the Christian to understand. The atonement of Christ in Scripture is utterly different than that presented by the Roman priest at Mass, and believers need to be fearless in presenting the truth of Christ's death to those who desperately need its powerful message.

The Once-for-all Atonement of Christ

If there is any one passage in Holy Scripture that is most relevant to the Roman doctrine of the sacrifice of the Mass, it is to be found in Hebrews chapters 9 and 10. Most works that oppose the error of Romanism find space for the citation of some of the verses from this section, showing that Christ's death is a completed, perfect sacrifice, needing no repetition, no "re-presentation" to be effective, and this is quite true. But most stop short of allowing the full weight of the text to be felt, for to do so would be to embrace the definite atonement of Christ over against the universal concept so prevalent today. We shall now look at this passage in the light of what we have seen from the Bible.

The writer of Hebrews begins in chapter nine by contrasting the old priesthood and its sacrifices with the new covenant in Jesus Christ. The old priesthood had many priests, he had asserted in chapter 7, for they were prevented from continuing their work by death. The new covenant is not like this, but has only one priest, Jesus Christ, who, since He abides forever, needs no replacement, substitute or fellow-worker, but is able to save to the uttermost those who come unto God by Him (Hebrews 7:23-25).[13] These priests came before God with the blood of goats and bulls, but Christ, on the other hand, has entered into the Holy Place with His own blood, and, in so doing, has obtained eternal redemption (9:11-12). He goes on to assert that a New Covenant has been made in the death of Christ by reminding his readers that a covenant is only ratified "when men are dead," that is, by death. Here is another difference between the atonement of Christ and the Mass, for we are told that Christ *does not die again* in the Mass, but His death is simply "re-presented." However, if there is no death, then there is no sacrifice, no renewal of the covenant. As he says in verse 22, there is no forgiveness without the shedding of blood. The Mass, being "unbloody," cannot provide forgiveness of sins as a result.

But the death of Christ is different from the old sacrifices. How so? The old priests had to offer their sacrifices often, yet Christ has died only once. The writer is explicit,

> "...neither should He offer Himself many times, as the high priest enters the holy

> place yearly with blood that is not his own. Otherwise, He would have had to suffer often since the foundation of the world; but now once for all at the consummation of the ages He has been manifested to put away sin by His sacrifice."

Sin *has been put away* by the sacrifice of Christ, hence He does not need to "suffer often". One sacrifice, effective as it is, is enough. There is no repetitive suffering on Christ's part, no being made present upon an altar "a thousand times" by a priest as claimed above by Catholic writer John O'Brien.[14]

The powerlessness of the old sacrifices, seen in their repetitive nature (just as the Catholic Mass!) is presented in Hebrews 10:1-3:

> "For the law, having only a shadow of the good things to come but not the very reality of things, can never by the same sacrifices offered year after year (which they offer continually) make perfect those who draw near. Otherwise, would they not have ceased to be offered, since the worshipers would no longer have had a consciousness of sins, having once been cleansed? But in those sacrifices is a reminder of sin year after year."

The sacrifices of the old law, since they were but dim shadows of the true sacrifice in Jesus Christ, were incapable of *perfecting* those for whom they were made. If they could, the writer argues, then they would not have to be offered over and over again. The *repetitive nature* of those sacrifices shows their imperfection: a perfect sacrifice needs to be offered only once, for it accomplishes that which it intends, that being the perfection and cleansing of the worshiper. Instead, the repetitive sacrifices of the old covenant functioned as a *reminder of sin year after year.* The yearly sacrifice informed the people that their sin was still present, and they were not perfected as yet.

Could anything more clearly apply to the Catholic doctrine of the sacrifice of the Mass? The Mass is repetitive in nature, offered many times for the same intention. If it was truly a "re-presentation" of the sacrifice of Christ, then it would not need to be repeated again and again, but would accomplish its intention immediately. Instead, the sacrifice of the Mass, offered over and over again, functions just as the old sacrifices, which were equally ineffective, in being a reminder of sins each and every time it is offered. Indeed, terrible as it may be for a Roman Catholic to realize, by assenting to the repetitive offering of the Mass, he is placing the offering of Christ *on the same level as the offering of the blood of bulls and goats under the old law*, as the Apostle goes on to say, "For it is impossible for the blood of bulls and goats to take away sins" (10:4). Neither the blood of goats and bulls, *nor the unbloody sacrifice of the Mass*, is able to perfect those who draw near to worship.

The Apostle continues on with his theme, showing that by His coming and His offering of Himself, Christ "took away the first in order to establish the second" covenant. In light of this he writes,

> "By this will we have been sanctified through the offering of the body of Jesus Christ once for all. Indeed, every priest stands daily ministering and offering over and over again the same sacrifices, which can **never** take away sins. But He, on the other hand, having offered **one** sacrifice

> for sins **for all time**, sat down at the right hand of God, waiting from that time onward until His enemies are made a footstool for His feet. For by one offering He **has perfected forever** those who are sanctified...For where there is forgiveness of these things, there is no longer any offering for sin" (Hebrews 10:10-14, 18).

The offering of the body of Jesus Christ is *once for all*. All for whom it is *made have been sanctified thereby*. This is why it is not offered again and again, because such simply is not necessary. The offering of Christ is complete and finished, for its work is accomplished and done. The antithesis between the old priest and Christ is complete, for the old priest offers the same sacrifices over and over again, while the new High Priest offers one sacrifice for sins *for all time* and then, having accomplished His work, sits down at the right hand of God. The old priest is still standing, for his work can never be finished, for his offering is incomplete and imperfect, insufficient to its task. But Christ's offering is complete, perfect, and all-powerful, and hence when it is offered He sits down at the right hand of the Father, there simply to present His completed work in intercession for those for whom the sacrifice has been made. His sacrifice is *for all time*, for by it He **has perfected** all those who are sanctified. The atonement is powerful in accomplishing the perfection of God's people. And so, he can conclude, where there has been forgiveness of sins, there is no longer any offering for sin. If an offering is still being made, then there has not been real and complete forgiveness.

Can the reader appreciate how fully these words apply to the Roman doctrine of the Mass? We took the time to emphasize over and over again in reviewing the teachings of the Roman Church the specific aspects of the "sacrifice of the Mass" that are here shown to be utterly incompatible with the work of Jesus Christ. The Mass is offered many times for the same intention; the sacrifice of Christ but once. The sacrifice of the Mass does not immediately remit all sin, and the "measurement of the punishments of sins remitted is proportional, in the case of the living, to the degree of perfection of their disposition."[15] The atonement of Christ is not dependent upon the disposition of human beings at all, but rather **perfects those for whom it is made**—it does not remit *part* of the penalty of sin, but, since it atones perfectly for all sin, it removes *all the penalty* of sin as well, for, where sin is forgiven, no basis for punishment remains. The differences between the Mass and the atonement of Christ are so basic, so fundamental, that no one can possibly hold to the New Testament teaching and to the Roman belief as well. And, given the centrality of the work of Christ to the entire Gospel proclamation, it can be readily seen why the Reformers, and all who hold to Biblical authority, refuse to the Catholic system the name "Christian," for one cannot truly own Christ as Savior and Lord when one denies the complete efficacy and power of His atoning blood!

The Christian can present to the Roman Catholic a Gospel that is powerful to save. Rather than the Roman concept of an atonement that is represented over and over again, thereby "applying" the fruits thereof to the worshiper, or the popular idea of a universal atonement of Christ that saves no one, but is dependent upon man for its effectiveness, we can proclaim the **fact** that Christ *has saved* and secured forever the remission of sins and the sanctification of all those who are His. Rather than a cross which shows the *impotence of God* in that it fails to secure the salvation of those for whom

Christ dies, we can proclaim the *powerful Savior* who, in union with the Father, sovereignly draws men unto Himself, having accomplished full and complete pardon in their behalf. This is why we have stressed the "Reformed" doctrine of the atonement, that is, the definite, specific death of Christ, for this only can speak with clarity, conviction, and power to the Roman Catholic. It is fundamental to the Gospel of the sovereign grace of God, a Gospel that is not centered in man and his actions, but in the Eternal God and His mighty will. This is the message that can free the Catholic from the slavery of works and penances! The powerful Savior, who sits enthroned in glory, never to die again, **has finished His work in behalf of His people!** It is no wonder that the heavenly host can sing a new song to the Lamb of God, crying out,

> "You are worthy to take the book and open its seals!
> For you were slain, and purchased for God by Your blood
> Men from every tribe and tongue and people and nation!
> And you made them a kingdom and priests to our God,
> And they will reign upon the earth!"
> (Revelation 5:9-10)

The Flaw of Purgatory

We have seen, then, the falsehood of the doctrine of the Mass, and the denial it contains of the finished and final work of Jesus Christ. But we also took the opportunity of looking at the Catholic doctrine of "purgatory." We shall now, briefly, point out how it, too, detracts from the atoning work of the Lord Jesus.

The majority of the basis for our examination has

already been laid. We have read in Scripture that there is no way of remission of sins outside of the cross of Christ. All sin, *including all punishment thereof*, is taken away by the Perfect Substitute, Jesus Christ. To assert that there is *any way of satisfaction or propitiation outside of Christ is to separate oneself from the Christian faith*. The Mass does just this, as it is **not** the same sacrifice offered by Christ on the cross. How, then, does the doctrine of purgatory detract from the work of Christ?

The Council of Trent spoke of the sacrifice of the Mass as "rightly offered not only for the sins, punishments, satisfactions and other necessities of the faithful who are living, **but also for those departed in Christ but not yet fully purified**."[16] We also read of the concept of the *purification of the poor souls* in purgatory before they are allowed to enter into heavenly bliss. Hence, according to Romanism, a person can die "in Christ" and yet not be fully purified. Beyond this, the Church of Rome teaches that the sufferings of these souls are "expiatory," able to remove the "stain of sin" that clings to them. The phrase used was "suffering of atonement."[17] Hence, there is to be found in the suffering of human souls satisfactory or expiatory merit in God's sight.

In light of what we have seen from Holy Scripture, it is clear that this teaching is far from the truth. Not dealing here with the supposed Biblical basis for the existence of purgatory itself,[18] it is clear that the *concept* is contradictory to the Scriptural teaching on the death of Christ. Rome here presents yet *another way* of forgiveness **outside of the finished sacrifice of Jesus**.

First, the Roman Church teaches that a person who is "in Christ" can die "impure." This is directly contradictory to the teaching of Hebrews 10:14-18 as seen above! The Apostle taught that Christ *already had purified those who are sanctified.* If one is in Christ, one has the "righteousness of God" according to Paul in 2 Corinthians 5:21. How then can anyone maintain some kind of impurity on the soul of the person for whom Christ has become the substitute? Did Christ not carry *all of the sins and transgressions* of His people (Hebrews 2:17, Colossians 2:14)? Most assuredly He did. Hence, the whole concept behind the doctrine of purgatory, that being that there must be a place of purging before a person enters into heaven, misses the Biblical teaching that God's people *have been purified in Christ Jesus*, and stand holy and just in God's sight, clothed in the righteousness of Jesus Christ, not any righteousness of their own gained by suffering and punishment. This alone is sufficient for any believing person to dismiss as human fancy the entire doctrine of purgatory.

But there is more. The doctrine claims that there is a way of forgiveness of sins—expiation—atonement, that lies **outside of Christ**. How can it be said that the suffering of human souls is in any way related to the work of Christ? So, if the "poor souls" in purgatory receive forgiveness or expiation of their sins and punishments in purgatory, they do so without the application of the atonement of Christ. This is another example of the simple fact that in Romanism, the work of Christ is not just sorely misunderstood, but utterly done away with, replaced with a fiction, a shadow, that bears only a superficial resemblance to the real thing.

John Calvin recognized that the seriousness of the teaching of purgatory lay in its impact on the work of Christ. He wrote,

> "Let us, however, grant that all those things could have been tolerated for a time as something of no great importance; but when expiation of sins is sought else-

> where than in the blood of Christ, when satisfaction is transferred elsewhere, silence is very dangerous. Therefore, we must cry out with the shouting not only of our voices but of our throats and lungs that purgatory is a deadly fiction of Satan, which nullifies the cross of Christ, inflicts unbearable contempt upon God's mercy, and overturns and destroys our faith."[19]

Furthermore, the related doctrine of *indulgences* is seen to be just as antithetical to the doctrine of Christ. Christ did not die to create a "treasury of merit" that may or may not be applied to someone simply on the whim of the Roman Pope. His death accomplished its goal, not by creating a huge bank account full of merit, but by perfecting for all time those who are sanctified!

The idea that there can be *any merit before God outside of Jesus Christ boggles* the Christian's mind. All men are in need of the righteousness of God in Jesus Christ, including every single person on the list of "saints" in the Roman Church as well as the Virgin Mary. Mary stands before God without a shred of righteousness of her own, wholly and completely dependent upon the work of Christ. The concept that she would have any "extra merit" to place into some treasury is far from the teaching of the New Testament! And then when it is asserted that this non-existant "extra merit" can be applied for the expiation of sin and temporal punishments of others—surely the non-Christian character of such a teaching is beyond dispute! Calvin was direct in his description of indulgences:

> "Now these, to describe them rightly, are a profanation of the blood of Christ, a Satanic mockery, to lead the Christian

> people away from God's grace, away from the life that is in Christ, and turn them aside from the true way of salvation. For how could the blood of Christ be more foully profaned than when they deny that it is sufficient for the forgiveness of sins, for reconciliation, for satisfaction—unless the lack of it, as of something dried up and exhausted, be otherwise supplied and filled? 'To Christ, the Law and all the Prophets bear witness,' says Peter, that 'through him we are to receive forgiveness of sins.' [Acts 10:43 p.] Indulgences bestow forgiveness of sins through Peter, Paul, and the martyrs....What is this but to leave Christ only a name, to make him another common saintlet who can scarcely be distinguished in the throng?"[20]

Here then is the fatal flaw of Romanism: the Church of Rome teaches a gospel that is devoid of the all-sufficient and finished work of Jesus Christ, and therefore declares that there are ways of expiation, atonement, forgiveness, that are outside of and distinct from, the atonement of Jesus Christ. The Christian Gospel is the proclamation of the death, burial and resurrection of Jesus Christ. To add to this message *other ways of forgiveness* is to destroy the Gospel itself and to fall under the condemnation of Scripture in Galatians 1:6-9. If you are a Roman Catholic, allow us to warn you to flee such falsehood and run to the real and living Jesus Christ, who is not to be found in the tabernacle of a Roman church, or upon its altar, but at the right hand of the Father, enthroned in glory, presenting there His perfect and all-sufficient sacrifice. In Him is forgiveness of sins, in Him is eternal life.

Chapter 7
Twisting the Scriptures

The non-Catholic reader might, at this point, be asking, "how can an honest Roman Catholic read the Bible and still believe in such things as purgatory or the sacrifice of the Mass?" While such a question is quite understandable, in the light of the teaching of the Word of God, it must be remembered that Rome is not without its apologists, and there are certain passages of Scripture that, if isolated from the rest of inspired Scripture, can be twisted far enough to make it look as if these teachings of Rome are actually based in the Bible. Of course, for many Roman Catholics, it has always been enough that "the priest said it, so I believe it." In many nations in the world today, this remains the situation. However, in America especially, more and more Roman Catholics are looking for a Biblical basis for their faith. Thankfully, many of those who look to God's Word find release from the bondage that is Romanism, and leave the RCC for churches where the Word of God is preached and believed.

But for others, the testimony of the Word of God is not enough. The Roman Catholic Church has taught its people that Scripture alone is not a sufficient or safe guide in matters of religion. While the discussion of the inspiration and authority of Scripture is not our intent here, it is recognized that for many Roman Catholics, no one but those "properly appointed" by the Roman hierarchy have the authority or right to interpret Scripture. Hence, when a priest shows a passage in the Bible to a Roman Catholic and says "this means such and so," many are disinclined to look further, accepting the word of the priest. Many Roman Catholics are taught that the Bible is so complex, and interpretations so many and varied, that they must have an "infallible interpreter" to tell them what the Bible means. Surely for most, who are utterly ignorant of the Bible and have not made any serious attempt to study it or its background (the same could be said of many Protestant churches as well, of course), the Bible is a mysterious book. But, are we really to believe that the Spirit of God did such a poor job in directing and guiding the various writers of Scripture that we cannot make heads or tails of its message? And on the central issues of the faith, such as the death of Christ, are we to entertain the idea that we cannot determine the correct teaching of Scripture? Surely there are many interpretations around—but does this mean that the Bible is not clear in its teaching? When one discounts all those interpretations that accept human traditions as authoritative, as well as those who reject the authority, inspiration, and the resultant inerrancy of the text, you don't have nearly as wide a field of interpretation as at first. And, when one begins to ask which of those interpreters left has given the most serious study to the language and structure of the text, as well as the historical backgrounds, the range gets even smaller. That is not to say that differences do not remain. The point is that the idea that no one can figure out the message of Scripture is untrue. Most of those who claim that you need **them** to understand the Bible are trying to keep you from finding out a few things that are in the Bible but are contradictory to their own teachings. Beware the infallible interpreter!

Roman apologists are quick to turn to Scripture passages, especially when dealing with a zealous Christian who wishes to share the message of full forgiveness in Jesus Christ. The Roman Catholic who is searching may find this to be a stumbling block in their run to freedom. Hence, in this chapter we will look at some of the prime examples of "twisting the Scriptures" on the part of Romanism. We do not pretend that we will be able to even begin to address **all** of those passages used by Roman apologists. Rather, we will look at the major ones, and see if we can find a common thread of *misinterpretation* in the Romanist's use of them.

John 6 and the Eucharist

Nearly every Roman apologist bases his defense of the concept of transubstantiation and the Eucharist upon Jesus' words in John chapter 6. A brief review of some of the more popular works available show how important this passage is for the Roman case: John O'Brien discusses John 6 at the beginning of his chapter on the "real presence";[1] James Cardinal Gibbons does the same thing.[2] John Hardon uses John 6 as Biblical evidence in his discussion of the "real presence,"[3] as does Alan Schreck[4] and Karl Keating.[5] Obviously, then, Jesus' words are very important to the Roman position.

The specific utterance of the Lord Jesus under discussion is to be found in John 6:53-57:

> "Therefore Jesus said to them, 'Truly, truly I say to you, if you do not eat the flesh of the Son of Man and drink His blood, you do not have life in yourselves. The one eating My flesh and drinking My blood

> has eternal life, and I will raise him up at the last day. For My flesh is true food and My blood true drink. The one eating My flesh and drinking My blood abides in Me and I in him. Just as the living Father sent Me and I have life through the Father, also the one eating Me will have life through Me."

The Roman Catholic claims that any understanding that does not take these words *literally* (which would mean that this could only refer to the Eucharist as taught by Roman Catholicism), is engaging in "spiritualizing the text" so as to avoid a belief they don't want to hold. This charge is made especially in reference to "fundamentalists." After all, it is the fundamentalist who insists on the inerrancy of Scripture, so why should they have to spiritualize things away? Aside from the fact that believing in inerrancy does not mean that you automatically embrace an interpretive methodology of absurd literalism, does the Roman Catholic have a case here? Is the literal meaning of the text supportive of Roman teaching on the Eucharist? Does a person literally have to eat the flesh of the Son of Man, and drink His blood (even though the cup is not given to the laity at all times in Catholic practice), to have life in himself?

First, we must point out that the *literal meaning* of the text is not always the *clear meaning*. The term "literal" is capable of quite a range of definition. If it is pushed to mean *absurd literalism*, and we are forced to use this understanding of the text, then obviously the whole Bible is full of complete nonsense. Jesus claimed to be the door of the sheep in John 10; *literally* this means Jesus is a door, replete with hinges, knob, and maybe even a lock! And, of course, this would also have to mean that only sheep will be saved, not human beings, for He is the door *of the sheep*. No one misunderstands the most basic elements of language so completely as this. Everyone understands that Jesus is speaking *figuratively*, and in fact the *obvious* and hence *the literal meaning* of the passage is the one which recognizes the symbolism of the language used. Hence, if the passage itself shows us that the terms used by the speaker are meant to be taken in a figurative or symbolic way, the truly *literal* interpretation will take this into consideration.

John loved to pick up on the different ways the Lord Jesus used to communicate a point. He differs in this from the other gospel writers, for in John the same teaching will be presented in numerous different ways. Jesus is "the light of the world," (8:12), the "good Shepherd" (10:11), and the "true vine" (15:1). Jesus is not literally the sun in the sky, a shepherd of sheep, or a living vine. Yet, each of these descriptions tell us something about Jesus, when they are taken according to the plain intention of the text: as symbols. So, too, John likes to use different phrases to say the same thing. One which is important in John 6 is his use of the phrases "have eternal life" and "shall be raised up on the last day." It would be an obvious mistake to differentiate between these two phrases. They mean the same thing, and are used in parallel to one another.

With these things in mind, we come to the longest chapter in the Gospel of John, chapter 6. John begins by narrating the miracle of the feeding of the 5,000 with the five barley loaves and two fishes. The people respond to this by saying, "This is truly the Prophet, the one coming into the world" (6:14). Jesus perceives that they are about to attempt to make Him king by force, so He goes away into the mountain by Himself. This is followed by the miracle of Christ's walking upon the water and calming the storm, which brings Him and His disciples to shore near Capernaum. The crowd, which has stayed the night near the place of their miraculous feeding, comes to Capernaum also, seeking Jesus. When they find Him, they ask Him how He got there, but the Lord brushes their question aside and gets to the heart of the matter. Jesus goes directly to their motivation for seeking Him. Remember that the night before they were going to make Him king by force. They are obviously mistaken about *who Jesus is*. The dialogue that follows will center on the *person of Christ* and His role in salvation. He turns their thoughts away from a secular kingdom onto His person, and the importance of their relationship to Him. Pressing the claims of Christ will result in many turning away from Him, but this is necessary to dispel false followers who are seeking nothing but their own benefit.

Drawing from the miracle performed the day before, Jesus in verse 27 says, "Work not for the bread which perishes but for the bread which abides unto eternal life, which the Son of Man will give to you; for this one the Father, even God, has sealed." The crowd was looking for a meal, but Jesus was directing them to Himself, the bread "which abides unto eternal life." The crowd does not fully follow His meaning, and asks what they should do to "work the works of God." Jesus' reply is that the work of God is to believe in the One whom God has sent, namely, Himself. This is quite a claim, of course, and the crowd demands a sign as evidence of His authority. They, too, grasp the aforementioned miracle, and assert that Moses had given them bread from heaven to eat. Can Jesus do the same? Moses had managed it for a long period of time, while Jesus did so only once. Can He do it again?

> 32. Therefore Jesus said unto them, "Truly truly I say to you, Moses did not give to you

> the bread from heaven, but My Father is giving to you the true bread from heaven, 33. for the bread of God is the one coming down from heaven and giving life to the world."

The quotation from Psalm 78:24 which is given by the people specifically identifies Yahweh as the "He" who gave them bread in the wilderness. Possibly they were referring this to Moses either directly or by implication, and hence Jesus corrects them. Either this or they are making the comparison between Him (whom some had said "this is truly the Prophet...") and Moses, and Jesus is correcting their misunderstanding of His person. Rather, the one source of the "true bread" is the Father—He gave the manna in the wilderness, but is now giving (present tense) the "true bread from heaven" which is not a perishable food but rather a person—"the one coming down from heaven." Again the magnitude of these words must be grasped. In each instance the former things, so precious to the people of Israel, is shown to be eclipsed in the life and ministry of Jesus, and even more so by His own person! The true bread is a person who has come down from heaven.

There is also another parallel (but an incomplete one, of course) —just as the manna came down from heaven and provided sustenance for the people of God during their sojourn, so too Jesus has come down out of heaven to be the sustenance of God's people—and their salvation. Jesus will utilize this kind of dualistic symbolism throughout this discourse, referring to the physical reality of the manna to represent the spiritual reality of faith in Him. Sadly enough, this dualism has been missed by the Roman church, which reads into this passage their own erroneous doctrine of transubstantiation in the Mass—and in so doing they reverse the very direction the Lord is taking the conversation. They, like the first century listeners, cannot see past the symbol to the reality beyond.

> 34. Therefore they said to him, "Always give us this bread!" 35. Jesus said to them, "I am the bread of life. The one coming to Me will not hunger, and the one believing in Me will never thirst.

The crowd continues in its blindness, unable to see the real significance of Jesus' words. Still recalling the feeding of the 5,000, they clamor for a continuous supply of the heavenly bread. In response Jesus gets quite specific—He Himself is this bread. The one who "comes to Me" - a clear reference to faith (as the parallel will show) will not hunger (hence, the bread is spiritual, not natural) and the one who "believes in Me" will never thirst. The reference to "thirsting" seems somewhat out of place here, given that only food has been in view up to this point; but in actuality there is no difficulty, as Jesus is not referring to actual physical consumption of food. He is referring to spiritual need. Man has a need spiritually (symbol: hunger and thirst) and Jesus meets that need completely and eternally. "Coming" and "believing" will become "eating" and "drinking" in verse 54. There is a clear progression in these terms, and to miss this, or to reject its meaning, is to miss the *literal* and obvious meaning of the text.

Following this, Jesus moves into demonstrating that no man can come to Him outside of the Father's drawing. In verse 36 Jesus brings up the subject of their disbelief, and in verses 37 through 46 He expands upon this topic. As this passage has been exegeted above in the chapter on the doctrine of salvation, we shall not restate those concepts here. Suffice it to say that the absolute sovereignty of God is placed before the people as the reason why some do not believe. This will become important to remember in verse 65 below.

> 47. Truly, truly I say to you, the one believing has eternal life. 48. I am the bread of life. 49. Your fathers ate the manna in the wilderness and died. 50. This is the bread which has come down from heaven, in order that anyone who eats of Him should not die. 51. I am the living bread which came down from heaven. If any eats of this bread he will live forever, and the bread is My flesh which is given for the life of the world.

The one who believes, Jesus says, has (present tense, continuous action) eternal life. Eternal life is not simply duration of life, but quality of life as well; not something just future, but present, too. But what is the person "believing"? Faith in the Bible always has an object—it never exists in a vacuum—faith is not a separate entity with an existence of its own. It seems that, in the context, the main object of faith is the person of Jesus Christ Himself. This is seen in a few ways. First, in verse 46 He speaks of being the "one who is from God." In verse 48 He speaks of being the bread of life. Both of these statements are assertions about who Jesus is—and hence are fitting objects of faith. Upon the assertion again of His being the bread of life, we seem to be re-entering the original conversation after having digressed (needfully) in regards to where real faith comes from—the Father. Jesus now resumes the pursuit of the original topic. The fathers of the exodus ate the manna in the wilderness and died, but the bread which comes down from heaven (Himself) is vastly superior (picking up the earlier comparison between the manna and His own miracle of the feeding of the 5,000) to the manna which was simply a picture of what comes later in Christ. The one who "eats" of this bread will never die. The "eating" here is paralleled with the "believing" of verse 47—any attempt to make this a physical action misses the entire point being made by the Lord. He who believes has eternal life—he who eats of the true bread from heaven will never die. Eating = believing. This is clearly the *literal* meaning of the text.

This faith is a personal one, because it involves the "eating" of this true bread—which is Jesus Himself (v. 51). The eating of the true bread means eternal life, and this bread, Jesus says, is His flesh "which is given for the life of the world." It is not Jesus' flesh, per se, which is the object here. It is His flesh as given in sacrifice which brings eternal life. It is the sacrifice that gives life, not simply the flesh. In His giving of His life, the Son provides life for the world. The context again demands a strict interpretation of "world". John uses "world" in many different ways, but here it is clear that the world is just those who are drawn by the Father, given by the Father to the Son, and who respond by faith in the Son. Consistency demands the continued emphasis on this group.

> 52. Therefore the Jews quarreled among themselves saying, "How is He able to give to us His flesh to eat?"

The Jews, continuing to dwell simply on the physical plane, and refusing to follow Jesus above to the spiritual truth underlying the symbol of His words, begin to quarrel among themselves about this. The men ask how Jesus can give His flesh for them to eat. Of course, Jesus is not saying that He is going to do so. He is speaking of His coming sacrifice and the resultant forgiveness of sins and eternal life for all who are united to Him.

> 53. Therefore Jesus said to them, "Truly truly I say to you, if you do not eat the flesh of the Son of Man and drink His blood, you do not have life in yourselves. 54. The one eating My flesh and drinking My blood has eternal life, and I will raise him up at the last day.

Jesus decides to come down to their level in an attempt to bring them up to His. He moves on with the metaphor, already firmly established, of "eating=believing". The only way to eternal life is through union with the Son of Man. This involves a vital faith relationship with Him, symbolized here by the eating of His flesh and the drinking of His blood. To make the equation complete, Jesus places "eating My flesh and drinking My blood" in the exact same position as hearing His word and believing on Him who sent Jesus in John 5:24, or as being drawn by the Father in 6:44, or as looking to the Son and believing in 6:40, or simply believing in 6:47. The result is the same in each case—eternal life, or being raised up at the last day. Hence, we here have a clear indication of Jesus' usage of the metaphor of "eating His flesh and drinking His blood" in John 6. Graphically we would have:

"All the ones looking upon the Son and believing" (6:40)
Those who are "drawn" by the Father (6:44)
He who believes in Christ (6:47)
"The one eating My flesh and drinking My blood" (6:54)

ALL EQUAL =

"eternal life"
or
"raised up on the last day"

Hence, the sacramental interpretation of this passage is left with no foundation at all. Jesus is obviously not speaking of some "sacrament" of the "Eucharist" supposedly established years later. His reference to His body and blood here is paralleled clearly with belief in the Son and the drawing of the Father, the same themes struck above. Consistency of interpretation must lead one to reject a sacramental interpretation of this passage. The *literal meaning*, given the parallelism already firmly established in this passage, has to refer to the union of the believer by faith with Jesus Christ, **not a participation in the Roman Catholic Mass**.

> 55. For My flesh is true food and My blood is true drink. 56. The one eating My flesh and drinking My blood abides in Me and I in him. 57. Just as the living Father sent Me and I have life through the Father, also the one eating Me will have life through Me.

The reason that one will have eternal life through feeding on the Son is simply that the Son is "true food and drink. He is the sole source of true spiritual sustenance. It is by vital faith that one is united with Christ (John 15:4-8). This is where life is to be found. Apart from Christ, the believer can do nothing (15:5) for Jesus is the source of all life. Life comes from the Father; it is given to us in the Son and is ours only in and through Him. As we know that eternal life comes by faith, then the eating and the drinking is a symbol of the continuous reliance in faith upon Christ. Here is the key to Christian life—reliance up the Lord Jesus Christ in all things. There is no other path to eternal life.

> 58. This is the bread which came down from heaven which the fathers did not eat

> and they died. The one eating this bread will live forever." 59. These things He said in the synagogue while teaching in Capernaum.

This fantastic discourse ends with the solemn warning: the fathers did not eat of this bread, and they died. Will His hearers understand this warning? John will tell us that all but a very few (and those only being the ones chosen by God) hear and believe. Men will continue to seek the natural, the physical bread, and ignore the true spiritual bread offered in Jesus Christ.

> 60. Therefore hearing this, many of his disciples said, "This is a harsh saying, who is able to hear it?" 61. And Jesus, knowing in Himself that His disciples were grumbling concerning this said to them, "Are you scandalized by this? 62. Therefore what if you see the Son of Man ascending to where He was before?

It is sad to see John's usage of the term "disciple" here. Many had followed after Jesus in a way that could be called "discipleship" but which was not a heart-felt conviction. There was no drawing or enablement of the Father within them. They were "scandalized" by the harshness of Jesus' words. Many people are. Many hate the strong teaching of the Bible. Their question, "who is able to hear it," goes to John's double usage of the word "hear" in his gospel. Only those who "hear" from the Father and learn from Him have eternal life.

Jesus knows the thoughts of these surface followers and asks them a simple question: if they are scandalized by these basic truths about His person, what are they going to do if they see Him in His glory -- the very glory He shared with the Father before the world came into existence (John 17:5)? Surely this would be even more difficult for them to handle. As Jesus said to Nicodemus, "If I speak to you of earthly things and you do not believe, how, when I speak to you of heavenly things, shall you believe?"

> 63. It is the Spirit which gives life; the flesh profits nothing. The words which I have spoken to you are spirit and they are life. 64. But there are certain of you who do not believe." For Jesus knew from the beginning who it was who did not believe and who it was that would betray Him.

There may indeed be a note of exasperation in Jesus' voice here. Can not even these "disciples" understand the difference between spirit and flesh? Have they not followed the obvious duality here? It is the Spirit which gives life—the flesh is of no use. These words of Jesus are spirit and life, yet they do not understand, because they do not believe. Jesus knew who didn't believe just as He knew who would betray Him.

> 65. And He was saying, "Because of this I said to you that no one is able to come to Me except it is given to him by the Father." 66. Because of this many of His disciples went away to the things behind, and no longer walked with Him.

The imperfect tense of the verb here indicates a continued action (or probably an iterative action in this case) in the past: Jesus did not just once say this to them, but often—"no one is able to come to Me except it is given to him by the Father". Some translations say "unless the Father enables him." Coming to Christ is not something that is the result of persuasive speaking.

Jesus was the greatest speaker of all time, yet many of His disciples "went away from following Him and no longer walked with Him." If man could be convinced in this way, these men would have been. But the operative factor was missing—the enablement of the Father. These "disciples" went away, not because of Jesus' words about "eating His flesh" or "drinking His blood," but because Jesus asserted that it is simply not possible for anyone to come to Christ unless the Father enables him. Roman Catholic writers continuously assert that these people went away because they would not accept Jesus' teaching on the Eucharist, the necessity of eating His flesh and blood. But what caused them to stumble was the proclamation of the absolute sovereignty of God, and the inability of man. The text specifically says, "**because of this many of His disciples went away...**" The topic of John 6 is not the Eucharist, but Jesus Christ; not eating the literal flesh of Christ, but being united to Him by faith, and receiving eternal life as the result. *A consistent, full reading of the text simply will not allow the Roman perspective to claim the name "literal" for it is anything but.* The Roman Catholic interpretation does dire damage to the context and meaning of the words of the Lord Jesus Christ.

"This is My Body"

On the night of His betrayal, the Lord Jesus left to His Church a memorial of His death, the Lord's Supper, so that by partaking in this supper, we might "proclaim the Lord's death until He comes" (1 Corinthians 11:26). The believer is well aware of the solemnity of the celebration of the Supper, and the special closeness to his Lord that is experienced during that time. The "words of institution" of this ordinance of the Church are special to all who call upon the name of Jesus. Matthew records them for us,

> "And while they were eating, Jesus took bread and, having blessed it, He broke it and gave it to His disciples saying, 'Take, eat; this is My body.' And having taken a cup and blessed it He gave it to them saying, 'Drink from it, all of you, for this is My blood of the covenant which is poured out for the forgiveness of sins.' "

We have already seen the Roman interpretation of these words in our examination of the doctrine of the Mass. The teaching goes so far as to say that *at the very time the Lord spoke these words, He was offering up a sacrifice to God, and the elements (the bread and wine) were already changed into His body and blood.* Of course, the RCC asserts that anything but a literal interpretation of the phrases "this is My body" and "this is My blood" is to attempt to avoid acknowledging the plain teaching of Scripture. But again, *is this the plain teaching*? Does an honest reading of the Lord's words **force** us to believe that Christ changed the bread and the wine into His body at this time, and then instructed His followers to do the same?

The Apostle Paul also spoke of that night, and the institution of the Lord's Supper. He tells us in 1 Corinthians 11:23-31:

> "For I received from the Lord what I also delivered to you: the Lord Jesus, on the night He was betrayed, took bread, and having blessed it, He broke it and said, 'This is My body [which is given] in your behalf; do this as a remembrance of Me.' Likewise also after the supper He took the cup, saying, 'This cup is the new testament in My blood; do this, as often as you

> drink, as a remembrance of Me.' For as often as you eat the bread and drink the cup, you demonstrate the Lord's death until He comes. Whosoever, therefore, eats the bread and drinks the cup unworthily, shall be guilty of the body and blood of the Lord. But let each man test himself and thus eat of the bread and drink of the cup. For the one eating and drinking [unworthily] eats and drinks damnation to himself, not discerning the body.[6] For this reason many among you are weak and sickly, and some sleep. But if we judge ourselves correctly, we should not be judged."

Here, then, are two witnesses to the institution of the Lord's Supper. Are we forced, by the words themselves, to understand this in the way the Roman Church teaches?

First, we must recognize the function of symbolic language in Scripture. We have already seen the use of it by our Lord in John 6. Some Roman apologists quickly assert that it would be highly improbable that the Lord Jesus, on such a serious and vital occasion as this, would risk being misunderstood through the use of "non-literal" language. Yet, it is on the very same night that Jesus gives the discourse to the disciples that is found in John 15, where He says, "I am the vine, you are the branches." No one asserts that He was being absurdly literal here, and this writer knows of no religious groups that teach that Jesus literally became a vine with branches by making this statement. Unless the Roman apologist wishes to argue that the content and message of John 15 is unimportant, the fact that the Lord was willing to use symbolic language at this time, and that He expected His disciples to understand it in that way, derails the objection to the Lord's use of symbols at this time.

The texts themselves provide further basis for the symbolic interpretation of the words of the Lord. Both Matthew and Paul record the fact that the blood of which the Lord Jesus speaks is the "blood of the covenant" or the "new testament (covenant) in My blood." The Scriptures are unanimous in saying that the blood of the new testament is the blood of the cross; and, as we have already shown that the sacrifice of Christ on the cross was a one-time, never to be repeated, complete and perfect action, then there is simply no reason at all to assume that these words carry any other meaning than to communicate the *representation* of the blood of Christ *soon to be shed at Calvary*. As these very apostles taught that it was the blood of Christ alone that is the basis of the new covenant, we should accept their testimony.

Furthermore, we see that even after the supposed "consecration" the Lord, and Paul after Him, continue to refer to the elements as *bread and wine, not as the body or blood of Christ!* When Jesus refers to the cup, He says, "I will not drink again of **this fruit of the vine** until that day when I drink it new with you in the kingdom of My Father" (Matthew 26:29). One can see the Lord Jesus, still holding the cup, and referring to it as He speaks. But what does He say? Does He say it is literally blood? No, He says it is the fruit of the vine, being even more specific by saying *this* fruit of the vine. And then He says He will not drink of it again until He would drink it with the disciples in His Father's kingdom. What is this? Will Jesus still be transubstantiating wine into His blood in the kingdom of God? For what purpose? Such makes no sense at all. Yes, of course we are looking at the text very closely, very literally, but is this not what is demanded by the Roman position? If we are forced to take "this is My blood" with the literality of Romanism, we have proper ground to point out the contradictions that arise as a result of their faulty method of interpretation. When such a methodology of interpretation results in absurdities in the text, then we know we've made an error.

Paul, too, refers to the bread, *after the blessing*, not as the body of Christ, but as bread. He says that "as often as you *eat the bread and drink the cup*" we demonstrate the Lord's death until He comes. He did not say we eat the body of Christ, or drink His blood.[7] When the person eats and drinks unworthily, it is said that he is eating bread and drinking of the cup. Each time it is bread and wine, not body and blood. But what of his comments immediately thereafter, where he speaks of not "discerning" or "recognizing" the body of the Lord? Does this require us to believe that the bread and the wine are literally the body and blood of the Lord? Only if we believe that a symbol is meaningless and trite. If we do not, but accept the seriousness of the Lord's Supper, without jumping to absurd literalism, we can see how the behavior of the people in Corinth was a sin against the institution and purpose of the Supper of Christ. Participation in the Supper is meant to be a memorial (*not* a sacrifice) of the death of Christ, not a drunken party as it had become at Corinth. In that light, a person's misunderstanding of the Supper would be a serious sin, as Paul explains. But to take this to mean that the bread and the wine are literally the body and blood of Christ in the Roman sense is to go far beyond the text.

We must remember that the use of figures or symbols is widespread in Scripture. In nearly every single instance, the Roman interpretation recognizes the symbol, and does not ask for absurd literalism. When Paul tells us in 1 Corinthians 10 (only a chapter before our text above) that the rock from which the Israelites drank "**was Christ**" (10:4),[8] are we to take this symbolically, or literally? Is Christ actually, in reality, truly and substantially, a rock? When Paul speaks of the Israelites being "baptized into Moses" just before this, were they literally baptized in Moses? Did they drink "spiritual drink" in a literal sense? Pushing this kind of literality is obviously foolish, and in pointing these things out we are not intending to be humorous, despite the fact that the consistent application of the Roman position to other passages results in these kinds of things. By pointing these examples out (and there is hardly a limit to how many examples could be given) we are simply demonstrating the inconsistencies of the Roman interpretation. Since the *ultra-literalism* of the Roman Catholic understanding causes contradiction within the text, then it must be inaccurate, and should be rejected.

A symbolic understanding of Jesus' words, "*This is My body*" does not in any way reduce the importance of the Supper. We have already seen that the Roman Catholic doctrine of the sacrifice of the Mass is anti-Biblical, and casts great disrespect upon the finished work of Christ on Calvary. We have also seen the wonderful truth of the all-sufficiency of the atonement of Christ, to which we are called *in remembrance* by the bread and the wine. If we do as the Lord commanded, and call to mind His broken body and shed blood, and in thankfulness confess our complete reliance upon, and indebtedness to, the work of Jesus Christ, we are showing the greatest demonstration of the fruit of His death until He comes. Each time we break the bread and partake of the fruit of the vine, we are showing the unity that is ours in the only place that Christian unity can be found—in the Lord Jesus Christ. We are showing forth the fact that all Christians everywhere owe all that they are or ever will be to the work of Christ at Calvary. We *look back* to the cross for it is there that our redemption was accomplished. It is there that we received a full and complete remission of sins. We do not look at *another sacrifice*, or a *re-presentation* of the sacrifice of Christ. There is no need for this. It is a memorial supper, as the Lord said. We remember *what has happened*. We do not by remembering make what has happened happen again.

Therefore, the *plain meaning of the words of Christ* must be that which the disciples themselves would have understood at the time. They have just celebrated the Passover, which itself is *incredibly rich in symbolism*. Each of the items on the table was a symbol of something to the Jewish people, a *reminder* of their escape from Egypt by the hand of God. They were already thinking symbolically. Hence, when Jesus takes bread and breaks it and says, "This is My body," no one in the room thought that He had just changed the bread into the very body that stood before them. And when He said the wine was His blood, He explained that it was the *blood of the covenant*, which they would have understood against the background of the blood of the sacrifice which was sprinkled upon the people to ratify the covenant long, long ago.[9] The blood of the covenant was blood of a sacrificial victim, not a living person. Knowing this, the meaning of Christ's words are clear: His blood, shed on Calvary, is the blood of the new covenant. But, since Christ had not yet died at the time of the Supper, it is impossible for this to actually **be the blood of the new covenant!** If the Romanist wants to be an ultra-literalist, then he must take it all the way. This is the blood of the covenant, yet that is impossible since Christ had not yet died. Clearly, then, Christ is using the wine as a *symbol of the blood of the new covenant*, and the bread as a symbol of His broken body.

They have to be symbols, since the reality was not yet in existence! Christ's body was not yet broken, yet He breaks the bread[10] as a symbol of the breaking of His body; His blood is not yet shed, yet He speaks of it as shed. All of this was *pointing forward* to the cross, and for us, *points back to it*. The supper finds its substance, its fulfillment, in the cross and in nothing else. It looks to one sacrifice, and reminds us that it was there, *and there alone*, that our redemption was accomplished.

There is no need to belabor the point, since those who are not convinced by the testimony of Scripture will not be convinced by over-long arguments, either. As in John 6, the *plain meaning* of the text is not an absurdly literal one, but the symbolic one. Just as one will end up with fantastic ideas from the book of Revelation if one sticks to abject literalism, the Roman concept based upon the words of Christ in the institution of the ordinance of the Lord's Supper leads to superstition, and, worse, a denial of the finished atonement of Christ. The Lord's Supper is a memorial of what He did, not a sacrifice in and of itself.

Purgatory and 1 Corinthians 3

In the desperate and useless attempt to find basis for the belief in purgatory within the pages of the Bible, defenders of the Roman cause have latched on to two primary passages: 1 Corinthians 3:10-15, and Matthew 12:32.[11] Paul wrote in 1 Corinthians,

> "According to the grace of God which was given to me, as a wise master-builder I laid a foundation, and another is building upon it. But let each one be careful how he builds upon it. For no other foundation can be laid than the one which has been laid, which is Jesus Christ. Now, if a

> certain one is building upon the foundation (with) gold, silver, precious stones, wood, hay, stubble—each one's work will be made apparent, for the day will show it, because it will be revealed by fire; and each man's work will be tested by fire, of what sort it is. If anyone's work which he built remains, he will receive a reward. If anyone's work is consumed, he will suffer loss, yet he himself will be saved, but so as through fire."

The Roman Catholic views this as referring to purgatory, yet there is almost nothing in the passage that can be found to act as a basis for such a claim. The mention of fire seems to be about the only common concept between this judgment of believers and the Roman doctrine of purgatory (even though modern Catholic writers are quick to point out that the RCC has never *dogmatically affirmed* that there is a literal fire in purgatory). But aside from this, nothing can be found to substantiate a concept of purgatory. What is judged is *the sort or kind of works the Christian has done*. Sins, and their punishments, are not even mentioned. It is works that are judged and put through the fire. If a person's works withstand the judgment, the person receives a reward. If not, the person suffers loss—not punishment, loss—yet is saved, "but as through fire." The passage does not say the person goes through fire, or is punished, or suffers to make atonement for sin. The passage simply says that the Christian's works are judged for what sort they are, and if a person's works are found to be made of wood, hay, and stubble, those works will be burned up and the person will receive no reward. For the Christian, the idea of not being able to present to his Lord works that were done for the proper motivation, works that were built with gold, silver, and precious stones, is a terrifying one indeed. It is no light matter to stand before the judgment bar of Christ! Yet, we must strongly affirm that this judgment is *not a judgment relative to sin but to works and rewards*. The believer *has already been judged with reference to sin in Christ Jesus, and has passed out of death into life, never to come into judgment for sin again* (John 5:24). The believer's sins were judged in Christ Jesus. The remaining judgment is not about salvation, but is about reward. Therefore, this passage has nothing to do with purgatory or a suffering to make atonement for sins.

The other passage cited is found in Matthew 12:32. Here Jesus speaks of the sin against the Holy Spirit, and says,

> "And anyone who speaks a word against the Son of Man, it shall be forgiven him; but anyone who speaks against the Holy Spirit, it shall not be forgiven him, neither in this age, nor the age to come."

The Catholic says, "see, it is possible to have sins forgiven in the age to come, just as Jesus said. This gives some support to the doctrine of purgatory." Aside from the oft-repeated truth that sin is either forgiven in Christ Jesus or it is not forgiven at all, does the Roman Church have a solid position here?

Long ago the pastor of the Church at Geneva replied to the Roman claim on this passage:

> "When the Lord, they say, makes known that the 'sin against the Holy Spirit is not to be forgiven either in this age or in the age to come'..., he hints at the same time that there is forgiveness of certain sins in the world to come. But who cannot see

> that the Lord is there speaking of the guilt of sin? But if this is so, what has it to do with their purgatory. Since, in their opinion, punishment of sins is undergone in purgatory, why do they deny that their guilt is remitted in the present life?[12] But to stop their railing against us, they shall have an even plainer refutation. When the Lord willed to cut off all hope of pardon for such shameful wickedness, he did not consider it enough to say that it would never be forgiven; but in order to emphasize it even more, he used a division by which he embraced the judgment that the conscience of every man experiences in this life and the final judgment that will be given openly at the resurrection. It is as if he said: 'Beware of malicious rebellion as of present ruin. For he who would purposely try to extinguish the proffered light of the Spirit will attain pardon neither in this life, which is given to sinners for their conversion, nor in the Last Day, on which the lambs will be separated from the goats by the angels of God and the Kingdom of Heaven will be cleansed of all offenses.'"[13]

Hence Christ emphasizes the *impossibility of forgiveness* for this blasphemy,[14] not the concept that there is forgiveness for sin in the age to come. The "age to come" for the Jewish person referred to the final age, the "Day of Yahweh," and to say that there would be no forgiveness for that sin in that age to come is the same as saying "it is unforgivable, period!"

The very fact that these passages, which are clearly about things *other than* purgatory, have to be pressed into service by the Romanist, shows how very little is the basis upon which the Roman dogma stands. Indeed, were it not for "sacred tradition," the Roman Catholic would have no basis whatsoever for its teaching of purgatory. And, when the fact that the whole basic concept of purgatory (i.e., the concept of atonement for sins by suffering) is seen from Scripture to be diametrically opposed to the Gospel, the Christian then must reject this falsehood with the strongest revulsion.

Conclusion

As I stated at the beginning of the chapter, it is not my intention to address each and every Biblical passage that is used by various Roman apologists in their vain attempt to substantiate the Mass or purgatory from Scripture. **If the Bible is consistent with itself**, then, given the Biblical data already examined, wherein the unarguable fact of the sufficiency of the work of Christ was established, any passage the Romanist can dig up to suggest the opposite will obviously be misinterpreted and twisted to suit his own preconceived aims and goals. Surely, given the claim of Rome to be the "mother of the Bible" and to have the full power of interpretation, the wise person will look askance at Roman interpretations, coming as they are from one who does not bow to the authority of the Scriptures themselves, but views them as the property of the Church! But one who accepts the claims of the Word upon his life will be less likely to twist and contort God's holy revelation to his own fancy. It is difficult to believe that the Pope, who uses the very name of God the Father as His own (the "Holy Father," see John 17:11) is willing to submit himself to the Word in humility, and seek its true meaning, rather than twist it to his own ends so as to establish the position he has usurped.

Chapter 8
What Then Shall We Say?

It is hard for us today to imagine the courage that was required for someone like John Hus, or Martin Luther, or Ulrich Zwingli, to stand up in the midst of friends and relatives and say, "The Roman Catholic system, to which we have all bent the knee, is not teaching the truth of God! We must return to the Bible to find the truth!" We have hundreds of years of history behind us, thousands of lives of wonderful men and women of God who have walked the path before us. At the time of the Reformation the path of truth was so little traveled that it was overgrown with weeds. Brave men and women again began to walk the path, and called out for everyone else to follow them.

For men such as John Hus, this required their lifeblood. Hus went to the Council of Constance in 1414 under a promise of safe-conduct by King Sigismund. He went to tell the Council why he believed like he did, why he thought that only Christ was the head of the Church, why he believed that salvation was by faith in Jesus Christ, and that His death was sufficient payment for sins. Despite the promise of safe conduct, Hus was arrested and eventually brought before the Council on July 6th, 1415. He asked over and over again to be shown *from Scripture* where he was wrong. His entreaties were ignored. He was forced to sit upon a high stool, and a pointed cap with pictures of the devil and demons was placed upon his head. There he sat while the bishop of Lodi preached a sermon based in part on Romans 6:6, "that the body of sin might be destroyed."

Hus was led by an armed guard of 1,000 men to the place of his death. Philip Schaff tells the story:

> "It was midday. The prisoner's hands were fastened behind his back, and his neck bound to the stake by a chain. On the same spot some time before, so the chronicler notes, a cardinal's worn-out mule had been buried. The straw and wood were heaped up around Huss' body to the chin, and rosin sprinkled upon them. The offer of life was renewed if he would recant. He refused and said, 'I shall die with joy to-day in the faith of the Gospel which I have preached.' When Richental, who was standing by, suggested a confessor, he replied, 'There is no need of one. I have no mortal sin.' At the call of the bystanders, they turned his face away from the East, and as the flames arose, he sang twice, Christ, thou Son of the living God, have mercy upon me. The wind blew the fire into the martyr's face, and his voice was hushed. He died, praying and singing. To remove, if possible, all chance of preserving relics from the scene, Huss' clothes and shoes were thrown into the merciless flames. The ashes were gathered up and cast into the Rhine."[1]

Schaff tells us that when the story of Hus' death, despite the promise of safe-conduct, began to circulate, the Council was quick to declare that promises of safe conduct are null and void for "heretics."

Hus did not think the matters that have made up the bulk of this book were unimportant. He was willing to die for the Gospel. So, too, was Martin Luther as he left Worms after having appeared before the Emperor under the same kind of promise of safe-conduct that had led Hus to Constance. He expected to die at any time. He did not, but he was willing to do so for the truth of the Gospel. Indeed, one could write volumes about those men and women who have believed the Gospel so completely that they were willing to die for it—not just for believing it, but for holding to the truthfulness of it in the face of those who also claimed to believe the Gospel, but who denied its saving efficacy.

The modern Christian today has as his or her heritage the bravery and courage of John Hus and Martin Luther, Zwingli and Calvin. Here were men who believed that the purity of the Gospel was far more important than any person's opinion of them. These were men who truly loved, because they did not care about what men said about them, only about what God saw in their hearts.

To the person who knows nothing but the world and its way of thinking, the past chapters have been nothing but theological double-talk, another salvo in a war no one cares about any more, that is fought by little people with less vision. Of course, the world thought that of Jesus Christ and His Apostles as well. The natural man can have little taste for the things of God, and surely the purity of the Gospel is not high on his list of priorities, nor should we expect it to be.

For the Catholic, reactions to what has been said would be dependent upon how much he or she knew of

Romanism before picking up this book, and how dedicated he or she is to the authority of the Roman Church. I have met some who have a "take it or leave it" attitude when it comes to theology, and the specifics of Roman belief are not really important to them. Others, who are dedicated to the teachings of Rome, will respond either with disgust and rejection, based upon a pre-conceived acceptance of Roman authority, or, God willing, if they are of an honest heart, they will search the Scriptures to see whether these things are so (Acts 17:11).

Surprisingly, reactions will be the most varied amongst those who call themselves "Christians." It is extremely unpopular to say anything that would in any way smack of "dogmatism" in major sections of American "Christianity" today. For those involved in liberal churches, the reason for this is to be found in the fact that liberalism has jettisoned the concept of truth, and replaced it with a "personal experience" of existential proportions, which makes something "true" for the person, but maybe not "true" for somebody else. What is "true" is true only because the person "experiences it" as truth. Truth, then, becomes a feeling, not an objective reality. The liberal is left with an "experience with Christ," even though they cannot explain *who* Christ is or was, *what* He taught, or *why* anyone should bow to Him as Lord. Why? The authoritative Word of God, and the teaching and doctrine found therein, has been compromised, relegated to the heap of human literature, deprived of its position as the sole rule of faith. The liberal can't even begin to tell you about his own experience, let alone define truth. He has no basis for saying there is anything such as "universal truth," so, obviously, he is not going to be writing a book about Catholicism and saying "this is false teaching, and here is why..."

On the other end of the spectrum is a large portion

of conservative Christianity. These folks speak often of "love." Sometimes it seems they speak more about love than they do about Christ. For these, the most important thing is that we "love everyone." "Don't offend anyone!" we are told, "just love them, and don't worry about all that doctrinal stuff. Just love, love, love." If a person is brave enough to say, "now wait a minute, that person has believed a lie" the immediate response is, "oh, how unloving! How judgmental you are! Christ would never do that!" Aside from the fact that it seems these folks have never bothered to read the 23rd chapter of Matthew, the fact of the matter is that *if a person is willing to allow another person to be deceived and injured by false teaching, especially false teaching on the very Gospel itself, that person does not love at all!* Christian love is united with truth. "Love rejoices with the truth" Paul tells us in 1 Corinthians 13:6. If you remove truth from Christian love you no longer have Christian love at all.

The Apostle Paul surely loved those to whom he ministered. Yet, he would not survive long in many of the churches today that have succumbed to a tidal wave of what the late J. Vernon McGee called "sloppy agape." When he withstood Peter to the face in Antioch for his hypocrisy, he was not doing so out of a "judgmental spirit." He was, in fact, showing real, Christian **love!** How? He knew that Peter's actions could result in a compromise of the very Gospel of Christ that can set men free from sin. To compromise the Gospel is to destroy the Gospel, for there is only one Gospel that is the power of God unto salvation. Hence, when he defended the purity of the Gospel, it was like he was defending the only cache of medicine in the world that can save the sin-sick soul. It is hardly an act of love to allow someone to come in and corrupt a life-giving drug so as to make it ineffective and useless, is it? Would we be concerned about "offending" the person who was trying to destroy the drug that was meant to save peoples' lives? Hardly. And to extend the analogy further, what if people were going about, distributing a corrupted version of the drug, that was unable to save the people? If we knew this to be the case, would we not warn the people that they were being deceived? Only if we loved them. But they might get mad at us, especially if they like the person who gave them the false drug. So? What if they do get mad? If we truly love them, will we not still tell them the truth?

Yet, today, many who claim allegiance to Christ are seemingly willing to allow false gospels and false Christs go unchallenged, all in the name of "love." Jesus did not display that kind of love. He told the truth, and offended many in the process. The Apostles did the same thing. The Gospel of Christ is very offensive to lost people, for it shows them their sin and their need of a Savior. The day that we make our message "unoffensive" is the day we are no longer telling the truth, no longer preaching the Gospel.

A word to the Catholic reader...

The death of Jesus Christ accomplished the full and complete remission of sins for God's people. He is the perfect and complete Savior, who is able to save completely, forever, those who come to God by Him. He does not need your works, He does not need your penances. There is nothing you can do to *make* Him save you, *make* Him be merciful to you. You can only throw yourself upon Him and Him alone, trusting that He is sufficient to save you. You cannot cling to Christ while holding on to popes, priests, or saints. He demands full and total allegiance, and allows no rival, no intermediary. If you will be His, He must be your all, your only master. All who would claim to stand between you and

Him are impostors, set upon keeping you from salvation in Christ. They may not know that they are doing this, but they are none the less.

When you are faced with the decision of going to Mass, you will now have a choice to make. It is clear that the "sacrifice of the Mass" is not the sacrifice of Christ, and hence is a rival, a substitute set up to keep you from the real thing. The Mass does not glorify Christ, for it teaches falsehood about His death. If you willingly partake in it after seeing the teaching of God's Word, you are knowingly rejecting the finished work of Christ in favor of the incomplete and imperfect way of Romanism. No person who truly wishes to follow Christ can be part of a ceremony that mocks His death. Harsh words? Yes, but words that are meant to cut away the falsehood so that you can find the truth. *If what we have said is true, then the Mass is a blasphemy against the finished work of Christ, and must be rejected by any who would seek salvation in Christ Jesus.* It is in love—Christian love—that we force you to a decision. You cannot remain neutral in the matter. You cannot continue to participate while thinking, "well, I just don't have to believe all that is said." By participation you are giving your support. You must have nothing to do with that which denigrates the atonement of the Lord Jesus Christ.

If you are unsure about the accuracy of what you have read, then ask your priest. Look up the references in a library and take them to him and ask him to explain them. Can he? Can he tell you that the work of Jesus Christ is really completed and finished, when he also has to tell you that the Mass is propitiatory as well? Is that consistent? Read the Word of God for yourself. Don't be taken in by the excuse that you can't understand it—do you really think that the Holy Spirit of God is such a poor communicator that He must have the priest to help Him? Check it out for yourself!

If God is working in your heart, and has given you a desire to come to Christ and Christ alone for salvation, then *close* with Him. Exercise those gifts of faith and repentance which God gives to those whom He draws, and believe in Jesus Christ as Lord, and as Savior. Bow to Him and trust in Him. Then seek to glorify Him by uniting with God's people in a place where God's Word is magnified and taught. Yes, you may be scorned and ridiculed by friends and even family for your faith in Christ, but your Lord was willing to undergo the scorn of the crowds to die as the Substitute for you. Can you do less?

A word to the Christian reader...

In light of the Roman Catholic doctrine of the Mass and purgatory, and the fact that the Gospel of Jesus Christ is contradicted by these teachings, how then should the Christian respond to Roman Catholicism and Roman Catholics individually?

One must first differentiate between the *system* and the *person*. The evil of Roman Catholicism lies in a system, not, by and large, the individuals who are a part of it. Only a small percentage of Roman Catholics are actively involved in promulgating falsehood. The vast majority are simply deceived, led astray from the simplicity that is in Christ by a system of religious works and duties. *The vast majority of Roman Catholics have never heard the Gospel message!* They have heard much about Jesus and salvation, but they have not heard the *truth* about these things. This places a great burden upon the Christian who wishes to witness to those trapped in the Roman system, for this requires us to understand the "language" used in Romanism, and to carefully point out to the Catholic the differences in meaning in the language we are using. It simply cannot be assumed that the Catholic has an accurate understanding of the most basic Biblical terminology. The Christian must be ready to explain things so that they can be understood properly.

A precious few in the Christian Church today recognize that the Roman Catholic Church is a huge field of missions. Millions of precious people await the message of salvation in Christ Jesus. The Christian Church must again look at its message and take the Gospel seriously, and in so doing, seek again to free the servants of Rome by pointing them away from a Pope and unto Christ Jesus. Few things are more rewarding than speaking to one who has been burdened with his sin and the continual wrath of God in punishments and introducing Him to the Gospel of the grace of God. The all-powerful grace of God is a message that melts even the hardest heart by the power of the Holy Spirit. Oh that God would raise up thousands of Christians who are filled with the love of Christ, and are fearless to proclaim the truth of the Gospel without compromise!

It is the *system* of Romanism that we must oppose, not Roman Catholics as individuals. The Papal system is opposed to the Gospel of Christ. We have seen that the teaching of Romanism denies the completed work of Christ. It teaches falsehood about the Gospel on a grand scale, and leads people *away from*, rather than to, Christ. Whatever else may be wrong with Romanism—the concept of the Pope, priests, Mariolatry, the saints, etc. and etc., all these are not as important for the Christian as the simple fact that Rome does not have the Gospel. As we mentioned in the introduction, Paul anathematized the teachers at Galatia for simply adding what would seem to us to be minor things to the Gospel. Paul knew what we must acknowledge today—that there is only one Gospel, and it cannot be compromised. Christians cannot be in fellowship with Rome simply because the Roman system is not a Christian system. "Ecumenical dialogue" is not a possibility since there are no grounds upon which it can take place. There can be no unity with Rome, since Rome cannot change her beliefs without ceasing to be Roman Catholicism. Her decrees are "irreformable," and therefore her blasphemous teachings on the atonement of Christ cannot be abolished, cannot be done away with. She will always be the Roman system, and she will always oppose the saints of Christ and the work of the Christian Church in the world.

No one is arguing that it is not "easier" just to ignore the "doctrinal differences." We grant that very quickly. But what is just as sure is that to ignore the Roman Catholic teachings under the guise of "Christian love" or "ecumenical cooperation" is just as surely to deny the Gospel of Christ and to do despite to the atonement of the Lord. **There simply is no way to compromise on the Gospel and yet claim to be a Christian. The Gospel is what defines a Christian in the first place.** The role of the Christian Church is not to be sitting about discussing social issues with Roman priests; the Church must be proclaiming the Gospel of Christ to *all* who are lost, *including those in the Roman Catholic Church, priests and all!*

But, sadly, it would seem that the majority of the "Protestant" denominations, especially those who actually claim descent from the great Reformers themselves, have not the slightest inclination to be about the evangelization of Roman Catholics. They are too busy scrapping the Bible, junking the foundations of their own faith, and meeting in "ecumenical dialogue" with Rome. Why is our day the day of "ecumenism"? Why are Presbyterians, Methodists, Episcopalians and Lutherans joining hands with Roman Catholics? The answer seems simple enough, but it should break the heart of any Christian who loves Christ and loves His truth. You see, it doesn't seem to matter anymore what Romanism teaches—all that is just "doctrine." Many branches of the Presbyterian Church, the Methodist Church, the Episcopalian Church, and the Lutheran Church, do not even make a pretense any longer about believing in the absolute authority of Scripture. Terms like "inspiration" or "inerrancy" are not be heard in many of their seminaries in our land. The people are taught that the Bible is just a collection of myths, legends, and fables; it is historically inaccurate, internally contradictory, and scientifically naive. Is it any wonder, then, that the great doctrines of Scripture, such as the depravity of man, the sovereign grace of God, and the atonement of Christ, are not seen as being important any longer? We do not know of these truths outside of Scripture, and when the Bible is relegated to little more than a "good old book," what it says about man and his sin will very quickly be forgotten. History shows us that in the churches that today enter into dialogue with Rome, and co-operate with Rome, the Bible and its authority has been dashed upon the rock of liberal thinking, left without power, without a voice of its own. When the Scriptures are taken from the center of the Church, you may as well dig the grave, for death follows right behind. Nothing is more chilling to the Christian soul than to see the edifice of a church that has abandoned the faith. It is devoid of the life of the Spirit, and is little more than a skeleton waiting to be blown down by the first wind that comes by. And are we to be surprised, then, when churches such as these are unwilling to decry the errors of Romanism? Certainly not. Only those who hold to the Biblical Gospel are going to cry out with prophetic warning to those who are fast slipping away into the abyss.

A Call to Action

The Christian of today is blessed with more knowledge and more information about the Bible and its teachings than any previous generation. This is a great privilege, yet it is also a great responsibility. The believer must know what he believes, and why he believes it, not just so that he can responsibly share the Gospel with those who have been given a false faith, a false hope, but so that he can "give a reason for the hope that is within" yet with gentleness and reverence (1 Peter 3:15) to all men, no matter whether their faith be Catholic, Mormon, Jehovah's Witness, or the ever popular religion of man: humanism. Today's Christian simply cannot ignore the command of Scripture to be an apologist as well as an evangelist.

In particular reference to the Roman Catholic Church, the believer must think carefully about his faith. Are the popular presentations of the Gospel to which he has been exposed accurate? Are they consistent? Or are they self-contradictory? Is God glorified when we proclaim contradictions? Is His name honored when it is obvious we haven't even thought through our own message? When we decry the Roman doctrine of the Mass, pointing to its incomplete and imperfect sacrifice, are we at the same time making Christ's work dependent upon man's actions as well? Are we willing to embrace the Bible's teaching, expressed so clearly by the Reformed faith, and speak of the definite atonement of Christ that is able to do that which God intends? Or shall we cower before men, and the traditions of our own churches? It is not popular to speak of God's sovereignty and man's depravity. You might find yourself in hot water with people you had always counted as friends, fellow-believers. Is the truth important enough to you to cause you to stand firm in what you know to be true?

If you confess faith in Christ Jesus, and have read this book to this point, then you cannot simply sit upon what you have learned. There is hardly anyone who does not either have relatives or friends who are Roman Catholics, or who does not encounter Catholics in their every-day activities. Will you speak to them of the love of Christ? Will you proclaim the atoning work of Jesus? What a privilege to be called of God to share the word of eternal life with those who walk in darkness! We cannot save anyone—only God does that—but we are called to be faithful stewards of the mysteries of God. We evangelize out of love and obedience to Christ, trusting Him with the results. May God light a fire of love in your heart, first for Him, and then, infallibly, for His truth. And, once you have committed yourself to the Christ who is truth Himself, may your heart be filled with compassion for those who do not know the Savior. May you be blessed as you share the Good News of the cross of Christ with Roman Catholics and all other people.

Chapter 1 Footnotes

1 See William E. Lunt, **Papal Revenues in the Middle Ages**, (New York: Morningside Heights, Columbia University Press, 1934) 1:111-125.

2 We shall examine the doctrine of indulgences in particular at a later point.

3 See the discussion in Schaff, **The History of the Christian Church**, (Grand Rapids: Wm. B. Eerdman's Publishing Company, 1910), 6:756-761 for discussion of whether indulgences at this time were said to remit both guilt and punishment; the reader should note that the distinction in Roman Catholic teaching between the *guilt* of sin and the *temporal punishment* thereof shall be addressed at a later time.

4 See the discussion in Schaff, **History of the Christian Church**, 16:763.

5 As a sample of the corruption of the papacy at this time, a brief note on how Julius (Guilano della Rovere) became pope would be helpful: "He began his ecclesiastical career by following his uncle, Francesco, into the

Franciscan Order. He was made a cardinal when his uncle became Pope Sixtus IV in 1471. After the death of Sixtus (1484), Della Rovere managed by bribery to have Innocent VIII elected. Controlling the papacy until Innocent's death in 1492, he was forced to flee Rome when his enemy Rodrigo Borgia became Pope Alexander VI. Following Pope Pius III's brief reign, Della Rovere achieved his own election as Pope Julius II in 1503 by means of bribery and extensive promises...In 1506 the construction of St. Peter's was begun and a special indulgence was proclaimed to help pay for it. The main objective of Julius' reign was to establish the papal power by the restoration of the Papal States. By means of war, interdict, and excommunication Julius subdued Bologna and Venice. Creating the Holy League, he ended French power in Italy at Ravenna, in 1512. These activities earned Julius the name of Pontefice Terribile and made him the object of satirical writings..." *"Julius II"* in **The Westminster Dictionary of Church History** edited by Jerald Brauer (Philadelphia: Westminster Press, 1971) pp. 465-466.

6 For a better discussion of the whole situation, see Schaff 6:764-767.

7 See Schaff, 6:765.

8 As cited by J. H. Merle D'Aubigne, **History of the Reformation**, (New York: American Tract Society, n.d.), 1:247. The same document will be found in the one-volume edition of D'Aubigne, page 88.

9 These issues are addressed in **Answers to Catholic Claims** by James White, (Southbridge, MA: Crowne Publications), 1990

10 D'Aubigne, **History of the Reformation** (Grand Rapids: Baker Book House, 1987, originally published in 5 volumes in 1846), p. 245. See also Henry Sheldon, **History of the Christian Church** (Peabody, Massachusetts: Hendrickson Publishers, 1988, originally published in 1895,) 3:81-82.

11 William Cathcart, **The Papal System** (Watertown, Wisconsin: Baptist Heritage Press, 1989; originally published 1872), p. 137.

12 Calvin's influence did not become very widespread until after the initial meetings of Trent. Later papal encyclicals would condemn the specific aspects of Calvin's theology, though much of his teaching, being in harmony with Luther, was condemned by Trent.

13 The technical term worked out by the Schoolmen of the medieval period was the "accidents" of bread and wine remain, but without any natural substance, for that had been changed to the body and blood of Christ.

14 *"Doctrine Concerning the Sacrifice of the Mass"* from the Twenty-Second Session, Chapter II, as found in **The Canons and Decrees of the Council of Trent** translated by H.J. Schroeder, O.P., (Rockford: TAN Book Publishers, 1978) pp. 145-146, with anathemas on those who reject these teachings to be found on pages 79 and 149. Emphasis mine.

15 See the *"Decree Concerning the Most Holy Sacrament of the Eucharist"* Chapter V in **The Decrees of the Council of Trent** p. 76, and the appropriate canon and anathema on those who would reject this teaching on page 80.

16 This is mostly due to the fact that Melanchthon, who took the leadership of the Lutheran movement after Luther's death, backed off from Martin's strong statements on the subject.

17 "Vicar" means "substitute"; hence, "vicar of Christ" is the "substitute of Christ", the one who takes Christ's place on earth.

18 The abbreviation RCC will be used throughout this work, and no disrespect is intended by its use at all. It is simply a fact that the phrase "the Roman Catholic Church" takes a lot of space, not to mention time in writing!

19 We include in the term "evangelicalism" all those denominations or sects which would identify themselves as "fundamentalists".

20 In saying this we are not even referring to the host of "Protestants" who have, in effect, denied their very heritage by denying the inspiration and total authority of the Word of God. It is with great sorrow that we say that entire denominations, which once stood for the Gospel of Christ have, over the last century primarily, abandoned their call, denied the Gospel, and have become, by and large, little more than social clubs. Many do not even deserve the name of "church." Those in such denominations will find little of interest in this work; my beliefs and theology are based on what they would consider the "old, outdated notions of fundamentalism" and, since such beliefs are obviously not worthy of "modern" consideration, little time will be spent pondering my perspective.

21 This is not meant as a blanket statement; there are

certain men who have extensive media ministries who also maintain a very high level of integrity and strive for doctrinal consistency.

Chapter 2 Footnotes

1 See **The Canons and Decrees of the Council of Trent**, pp. 29, 72 as examples.

2 These issues are addressed in **Answers to Catholic Claims** by James White, (Southbridge, MA: Crowne Publications), 1990

3 John Hardon, **Pocket Catholic Dictionary**, (New York: Image Books, 1985), p. 449.

4 Hardon, p. 271.

5 See Matthias Premm, **Dogmatic Theology for the Laity**, (Rockford: TAN Book Publishers, 1977) p. 327.

6 Ludwig Ott, **Fundamentals of Catholic Dogma**, (Rockford: TAN Book Publishers, 1974) p. 433.

7 Ott, p. 433, *"The Most Holy Sacraments of Penance and Extreme Unction"* from the Council of Trent, chapter 5 in Schroeder, **The Canons and Decrees of the Council of Trent**, p. 93.

8 See Chapter 15 of the Sixth Session of the Council of Trent, *"Decree Concerning Justification."* Schroeder, p. 40.

9 See Chapter 6 of the Fourteenth Session of Trent, Schroeder p. 95.

10 Fourteenth Session of Trent, Chapter VIII, Schroeder pp. 97-98.

11 Ott, p. 434.

12 This phrase is used often in the decrees of the Council of Trent to refer to baptism. See Schroeder, p. 22 for an example.

13 Schroeder, p. 33.

14 Canon 30 on the *"Decree on Justification"*, Schroeder, p. 46.

15 Schroeder, p. 39.

16 Ott, p. 264.

17 Compare this statement with Hebrews 10:10-17.

18 Premm, pp.262-263.

19 Schroeder, p. 29.

20 Schroeder, pp. 30-31.

21 Schroeder, p. 31.

22 Schroeder, pp. 31-32.

23 Schroeder, p. 34.

24 Schroeder, p. 36. See below for the discussion of the Biblical meaning of *"justification"* and how this differs greatly from the Roman concept.

25 Schroeder, p. 42.

26 John A. O'Brien, **The Faith of Millions**, (Huntington, Indiana: Our Sunday Visitor, Inc. 1974) pp. 142-143.

27 James Cardinal Gibbons, **The Faith of our Fathers**, (Rockford: TAN Book Publishers, 1980) p. 227.

28 Walter M. Abbott, **The Documents of Vatican II**, (New York: Crossroad Publishing Company, 1966), *"Constitution on the Sacred Liturgy,"* 1:6, p. 140.

29 Schroeder, p. 53.

30 Ott, p. 416.

31 Ott, p. 431.

Chapter 3 Footnotes

1 Matthias Premm, **Dogmatic Theology for the Laity**, p. 346.

2 Ludwig Ott, **Fundamentals of Catholic Theology**, p. 397.

3 **Vatican Council II, The Conciliar and Post Conciliar Documents**, Volume I, edited by Austin Flannery, (Northport, New York: Costello Publishing, 1984), *Directory on Children's Masses* 8, p. 256.

4 John Hardon, **The Catholic Catechism**, (New York: Doubleday & Company, Inc., 1975), P. 457

5 John O'Brien, **The Faith of Millions**, (Huntington: Our Sunday Visitor Inc 1974), pp. 255-256.

6 **The Canons and Decrees of the Council of Trent**, translated by H.J. Schroeder, p. 72.

7 Schroeder, p. 73.

8 Ibid.

9 Schroeder p. 74.

10 Latin for "according to the import of the words," that is, the words of Christ at the Last Supper.

11 Schroeder, pp. 74-75.

12 Schroeder, p. 75.

13 Gibbons wrote in **The Faith of Our Fathers** in regards to the Protestant rejection of transubstantiation, and the Protestant understanding of Jesus' words "This is my body" as non-literal, "Why is the Catholic interpretation of these words rejected by Protestants? Is it because the text is in itself obscure and ambiguous? By no means; but simply because they do not comprehend how God could perform so stupendous a miracle as to give His body and blood for our spiritual nourishment." No, the rejection has to do with both the text, which does not admit of such a literal interpretation, and the whole teaching of Scripture on the atonement. There is no question that *if* the Scriptures taught that this happened, then it could happen. The fact shall be demonstrated, however, that the Scriptures teach no such thing.

14 The highest form of worship in Catholic belief.

15 Schroeder, p. 76.

16 A modern Catholic document explains, "Pastors should ensure that, unless there is a grave reason against it, churches in which the blessed Sacrament is normally reserved should be open every day for at least some hours, at the most suitable times, so that the

faithful may be easily able to pray before the blessed Sacrament." (Flannery, I:244). Another writes, "Christ's presence in the eucharist in the tabernacle of every Catholic church is a way in which God today dwells among his people with special closeness. This is why our churches are open daily, why people often drop in for a 'visit' to share their joys and sorrows with Christ, or just to talk things over." (Anthony Wilhelm, **Christ Among Us**, (New York: Paulist Press, 1981) p. 252).

17 Schroeder, pp. 79-80.

18 John Hardon defines *immolation* as, "The actual or equivalent destruction of some material object as an act of sacrifice. When the destruction is done actually, the object is radically changed, as when an animal is killed or wine is poured out. When the destruction is not done but is equivalent, it is called mystical or symbolic, as occurs in the sacrifice of the Mass, where the separate consecration of the bread and wine symbolizes the separation of Christ's body and blood on Calvary." (Hardon, **Pocket Catholic Dictionary**, p. 189).

19 Schroeder, pp. 144-145.

20 Schroeder, pp. 145-146.

21 The many difficulties and contradictions this teaching presents will be addressed fully below.

22 The fact that it is impossible to be *in Christ* without being by virtue of that union fully and completely purified seems to have missed the attention of the Council of Trent. This Biblical teaching will be addressed under the Atonement of our Lord Jesus Christ below.

23 Ott, p. 414.

24 Ott writes, "As a propitiatory and impetratory Sacrifice, the Sacrifice of the Mass possesses a finite external value, since the operations of propitiation and impetration refer to human beings, who as creatures can receive a finite act only. This explains the practice of the Church of offering the Holy Sacrifice of the Mass frequently for the same intention." And he adds, "As the Sacrifice of the Mass does not work mechanically any more than the Sacraments, the receiving of the fruits of the Sacrifice demands certain due moral dispositions, and the measure of the fruits received is dependent on the quality of these dispositions." pp. 414-415.

25 As this canon states the thesis of this work fairly well, it is then clear that by taking the position we do, founded, as shall be shown, on the testimony of the Word of God, we are under the anathema of the Church of Rome; but, it is far better to be anathematized by men than rejected by God!

26 Schroeder, pp. 149-150.

27 Schroeder, p. 150.

28 Abbott, *"Constitution on the Sacred Liturgy,"* 2, p. 137.

29 Abbott, 7, pp. 140-141.

30 Abbott, 10, p. 142.

31 Abbott, 47, p. 154.

32 Ibid.

33 Abbott, 55, p. 156.

34 Abbott, *"Decree on Ecumenism,"* 22, p. 364.

35 Abbott, 3, p. 16.

36 Abbott, 11, p. 28.

37 Abbott, 28, p. 53.

38 **Vatican Council II, The Conciliar and Post Conciliar Documents**, edited by Austin Flannery, I:104.

39 Abbott, 3, p. 153.

40 Flannery, 2-3, pp. 154-156.

41 Gibbons, **Faith of our Fathers**, pp. 254-255.

42 Ott, p. 379.

43 Ott, p. 402. Ott says in this same place, "The serious accusations of the Reformers proceed from the false presupposition that the sacrifice of the Mass according to Catholic teaching, is an independent sacrifice side by side with the Sacrifice of Christ on the Cross, and that in virtue of the sacrificial activity of the priest it confers ex opere operato forgiveness of personal sins and punishments of sins." This is not exactly accurate; it lies more upon the assertion that the Catholic attempt to connect intimately the Mass and Calvary is not tenable either Biblically or logically.

44 Ott, p. 407.

45 Ibid.

46 Note especially Hardon's comment, "What the Church teaches is that, while the blessings of salvation were merited for mankind on the cross, they are still to be applied to us, principally through the Mass" (p. 468).

47 Peter Stravinskas, **The Catholic Response**, (Huntington: Our Sunday Visitor, Inc 1985).

48 William Ogrodowski, **A Catholic Book of the Mass** (Huntington: Our Sunday Visitor, Inc 1985).

49 Alan Schreck, **Catholic and Christian**, (Ann Arbor, Michigan: Servant Books, 1984).

Chapter 4 Footnotes

1 Schroeder, **The Canons and Decrees of the Council of Trent**, p. 214.

2 John Hardon, **The Catholic Catechism**, pp. 273-274.

3 See discussion above, and Ott, **Fundamentals of Catholic Dogma**, pp. 412-415.

4 Ott, p. 485.

5 Gibbons, **The Faith of our Fathers**, p. 173.

6 William Cathcart, **The Papal System**, p. 263.

7 See Ott, p. 188 on Christ's super-abundance of merit.

8 O'Brien, **The Faith of Millions**, p. 195.

9 O'Brien, p. 196.

10 O'Brien, p. 198.

11 O'Brien, p. 200.

12 Philip Schaff records that this phrase was said by Tetzel himself, recording it as
"Sobald der Pfennig im Kasten klingt,
Die Seel' aus dem Fegfeuer springt."
See Schaff, **History of the Christian Church** (Grand Rapids: Wm. B. Eerdman's Publishing Company, 1910) VII:153.

13 Schroeder, p. 254.

14 An excellent source of the traditions connected with purgatory is to be found in F.X. Shouppe's **Purgatory: Explained by the Lives and Legends of the Saints** (Rockford: TAN Book Publishers, 1986).

15 Shouppe, **Purgatory**, pp. 136-137.

16 Cathcart, pp. 264-265. See pages 264 through 268 for further tales of purgatorial suffering.

17 Walter Abbott, **The Documents of Vatican II**, *"Dogmatic Constitution of the Church"* 151, pp. 83-84.

18 Austin Flannery, **Vatican Council II, the Conciliar and Post-Conciliar Documents**, I:62.

19 Flannery, I:63.

20 Flannery, I:64.

Chapter 5 Footnotes

1 Indeed, as one Roman Catholic recently said to us, "...the Bible is *not* the authority for the Roman Catholic Church...But the Holy Church is, most definitely, the authority for the Bible."

2 The reader is directed to such fine works as A.W. Pink's **The Sovereignty of God**, or to John Calvin's **Institutes of the Christian Religion** for much fuller discussions of these issues.

3 As cited by A.W. Pink in **Gleanings in the Godhead**, (chicago: Moody Press, 1975) pp. 31-32

4 See Robert Morey, **Here is Your God** (Southbridge, Massachusetts: Crowne Publications, 1989) or A.W. Pink, **The Attributes of God** (Grand Rapids: Baker Book House, 1975) for excellent discussions of the nature of God.

5 Which, for the Catholic reader, does not take place at baptism but at the point of regeneration by the Spirit of God, baptism following *after* this in the New Testament.

6 See the discussion on John 6 below.

7 See the canons on justification in the **Council of Trent**, Schroeder, pp. 42-46, especially #4.

8 John Calvin, **The Institutes of the Christian Religion**, (Philadelphia: Westminster Press, 1960) Book III, Chapter 4, section 29, p. 656.

9 Calvin, **Institutes of the Christian Religion**, Book I, Chapter 4, section 30, p. 657.

10 That being an aorist subjunctive of strong denial.

11 The term "foreknown" (προγινώσκω, *proginosko*) as used here does not mean "to know (as in have knowledge of simple factual data) beforehand." A study of its background in the Old Testament and its usage here indicates that it refers to God's gracious choice to enter into relationship with a people or a person.

12 On this issue, see John Calvin, **Commentaries on the Epistle of Paul the Apostle to the Romans**, (Grand Rapids: Baker Book House, 1984), or **Concerning the Eternal Predestination of God** (Greenwood, South Carolina: The Attic Press, 1961)

Chapter 6 Footnotes

1 The King James Version utilizes the translation "atonement" of the Greek term usually translated "reconciled" (καταλλαγήν) in Romans 5:11. The actual rendering of "atonement" would not be *improper* for the term "propitiation."

2 Or "made righteous." The one Greek term δικαιόω (or the noun δικαιοσύνη) can be translated either as "to make righteous" or "to justify." To be justified is to be made righteous—there is no Biblical difference between the two translations.

3 See the excellent discussion in Calvin, **The Institutes of the Christian Religion**, Book III, Chapter 4, sections 26 and 27.

4 John's use of the term "world" here should be understood in the light of the parallel passage in his Gospel, 11:51-52, where it is clear that he is not referring to *every single individual person in the world*, but rather to *every different kind or type of person*, as he also wrote in Revelation 5:9-10 with reference to the atoning work of Christ, "...for You were slain and purchased for God by

Your blood men from every tribe and tongue and people and nation, and made them kings and priests to our God...." In each instance the emphasis is on the fact that the work of Christ redeems *all different kinds of men*, **not** that all indiscriminately are redeemed.

5 ἀπολύτρωσις, *"redemption, acquittal, also the state of being redeemed"* (**A Greek-English Lexicon of the New Testament and Other Early Christian Literature**, by Walter Bauer, edited by Arndt, Gingrich and Danker, Second Edition, (Chicago: University of Chicago Press, 1979) p. 96).

6 The contention that men are punished not for their sins, which are forgiven in Christ, but for their unbelief, will be dealt with below.

7 The intimate relationship between the *propitiatory work* of Christ and His *work of intercession* can be seen as well in 1 John 2:1-2.

8 John Owen, **The Death of Death in the Death of Christ**, (London: Banner of Truth Trust, 1985), p. 78.

9 And note that in John 6:39, after speaking of God's "giving" men to Him, Christ says that it is the Father's will that He lose *none* of those given Him by the Father. Hence, if those who are given to the Son in John 6 are the same as His sheep in John 10, then none of the sheep shall perish, but all shall be saved, or Christ does not always do the will of the Father, an unthinkable thing indeed. Hence, all those for whom Christ dies (the sheep) are saved.

10 The term πίστις can be translated either as "faith" or "faithfulness" as it is in some translations. In either

case it is the supernatural work of the Spirit of God.

11 The action of believing is a present participle (πιστεύων) showing continuous action in the present; the action of being born of God (γεγέννηται) is perfect in tense, indicating a past tense action. Hence, being born of God precedes the present action of belief.

12 "Particular Redemption" Sermon 181 in the New Park Street Pulpit IV, 135.

13 It should be noted that the Roman Catholic concept of a separate group of celibate priests who have sacrificial powers via consecration is not only utterly without basis in the New Testament, but is a blatant attempt to return to old-covenant concepts, and, as such, is an attack upon the finished work of Christ at Calvary, just as the doctrine of the Mass. When Christ died, the veil in the Temple was torn from top to bottom (Matthew 27:51), opening forever the access through His body into the Holy of Holies. Any "priesthood system" like that of Romanism or as found in the Church of Jesus Christ of Latter-day Saints (the Mormons) is an "undoing" of what Christ did that day.

14 See above, page 40.

15 Ludwig Ott, **Fundamentals of Catholic Dogma**, p. 414.

16 Schroeder, **The Canons and Decrees of the Council of Trent**, p. 146.

17 Ott, p. 485.

18 These proof-texts will be addressed below.

19 Calvin, **Institutes of the Christian Religion**, III:V:6, p. 676.

20 Calvin, **Institutes of the Christian Religion**, III:V:2,3 pp. 671, 673.

Chapter 7 Footnotes

1 John O'Brien, **The Faith of Millions**, pp.205-208.

2 James Cardinal Gibbons, **The Faith of our Fathers**, pp. 236-237.

3 John Hardon, **The Catholic Catechism**, pp. 458-459.

4 Alan Schreck, **Catholic and Christian**, pp. 128-129.

5 Karl Keating, **Catholicism and Fundamentalism**, pp. 232-236.

6 The phrase "of the Lord," found in many English translations, is not given by the Nestle-Aland 26th edition Greek text. In light of Paul's earlier discussion of the body of the Church eating one "bread" (1 Corinthians 10:16-17), some interpreters would here see the text as given by Nestle-Aland as referring not the body of Christ specifically, but His body, the Church.

7 Indeed, if absurd literality is the mode of the day, we might point out that, to be consistent, the Catholic

should drink the literal cup, not just its contents, as that is the *literal* way it reads. No one would accept such an absurdity, yet the Protestant is the one charged with being inconsistent in his interpretation.

8 For those Roman apologists who pride themselves on the meaning of the Greek verb ειμί (*eimi*), asserting that it **must** be taken literally in Matthew 26:26, etc. we might point out that in 1 Corinthians 10:4 the verb is ἦν (*en*), the imperfect or aorist form of ειμί. Hence, if we have to take it *literally* in one place, consistency demands we take it *literally* everywhere else.

9 Exodus 24:8.

10 Many manuscripts of I Corinthians 11:24 read, "My body *which is broken* for you..."

11 To attempt to establish a custom of praying for the dead, as Catholics do for those supposedly in purgatory, the apocryphal book of 2 Maccabees (12:43-46) is cited. While not even attempting to deal with the whole passage (recognizing that this author finds no solid basis for believing this book to be Scripture, as the Lord Jesus and His Apostles did not seem to view it as such), it should be pointed out that simply establishing prayers for the dead **does not establish purgatory**. One could pray for the Lord's mercy upon a dead person without thinking that there was some "intermediate" state wherein the person was undergoing punishment. This is especially so for the New Testament writers, for the whole concept of a person dying "impure," as we saw above, is antithetical to their teaching on the sufficiency of the work of Christ.

12 Likewise, blasphemy of the Holy Spirit is obviously a

"mortal sin" in Catholic understanding, and hence no person guilty of this would be in purgatory in the first place, as *guilt or eternal punishment* cannot be remitted, according to Catholic dogma, in purgatory.

13 John Calvin, **Institutes of the Christian Religion**, Book III, Chapter 5, section 7, p. 677.

14 The "unpardonable sin" is understood in many ways. It is clearly the blasphemy of the Holy Spirit. But what makes it unpardonable while blasphemy against the Son of Man is not? May we suggest that the sin is to be understood in the light of the fact that it is the Holy Spirit who brings spiritual life and light to the sinner. If one blasphemes the Spirit (as the Jews had just done by attributing the work of the Spirit to the operation of Satan), one is obviously giving evidence of not being under the Spirit's influence. One in whom the Spirit is working would never do this, and indeed it seems that one in whom the Spirit ever *intends to work* would not be allowed to so blaspheme. Therefore, such a person who is so twisted as to call light darkness and darkness light is devoid of the Spirit, and hence unable to even seek after or ask for pardon, as the Spirit is the only source of that conviction that would lead one to repentance. Hence, it is not the *seriousness* of the sin that is in view (as if the blood of Christ were insufficient to cleanse from it), but the *effect upon the sinner* and the position of the sinner that it indicates.

Chapter 8 Footnote

1 Philip Schaff, **History of the Christian Church**, 16:382-383.

Also Available from

Crowne Publications, Inc.

When Is It Right To Fight - Dr. Robert A. Morey

Christian pacifism is examined as a controversial issue. Peace cannot always be the Christian response to the evil that men do.

143 pages

Battle Of The Gods - Dr. Robert A. Morey

Today, God's character and attributes are being called into question. Some well-known theologians have resurrected neo-pagan views of God and have tried to pass them off as Christian. **Dr. Morey has written the definitve rebuttal to the "God as finite" view.**

316 pages

Studies In The Atonement - Dr. Robert A. Morey

This book, which is a fine statement on the doctrine of the atonement, should be read by every Christian, pastor and teacher. It is comprehensive, readable, pracitical and Scriptural

336 pages

A Layman's Guide to the Lordship Controversy by Dr. Richard P. Belcher

Here is a book that clearly summarizes the two viewpoints of lordship and nonlordship salvation, then compares them in the areas and theology and exegesis, and finally critiques the nonlordship position in its arguments, theology and exegesis.

128 pages

A Journey In Grace by Dr. Richard P. Belcher

This is the story of a young pastor with a typical twentieth century theology and his pursuit of a burning theological question which was triggered in his first experience with a pulpit search committee. He cannot and does not rest until he has answered the challenge of the question, "Young man, are you a Calvinist?"

154 pages

Tablets of Stone - John G. Reisinger

A study of the nature and function of the Ten Commandments in the history of redemption as they relate to the nation of Israel and the Christian Church.

120 pages

But I Say Unto You,... - John G. Reisinger

A very thorough study of the contrasts found in the Sermon on the Mount between the life of an Israelite under law and the life of a Christian under grace.

112 pages

Sovereignty Of God In Providence - John G. Reisinger

A Biblical study of six basic principles that undergird all of Scripture as it relates to human destiny and God's sovereign providence.

40 pages

I Believe in Inerrancy by Dr. Richard P. Belcher

A biblical, historical and theological presentation of the doctrine of the inspiration of Scripture.

54 pages

A Layman's Guide to the Inerrancy Debate by Dr. Richard P. Belcher

A series of essays answering key questions and objections concerning the doctrine of Biblical inerrancy.

80 pages

Arthur W. Pink - Predestination by Dr. Richard P. Belcher

An analysis and critique of the central theological theme of A.W. Pink. This work uses the Pink sources to set forth his views of predestination, election, and reprobation.

136 pages

A Comparison of Dispensationalism and Covenant Theology by Dr. Richard P. Belcher

An objective analysis and comparison of these two major systems of theology.

46 pages

Worship Is All Of Life - Dr. Robert A. Morey

The most complete study of worship in this century. This book reveals everything you wanted to know about worship from personal devotions, family worship and public worship. Chosen as "the best of good books" by the Christian Booksellers Association.

113 Pages

The Impossibility Thinking of Robert Schuller by Dr. Richard P. Belcher

An analysis and critique of the theology of Robert Schuller's best-selling book on self-esteem concluding that Schuller's thinking is neither Biblical nor historically Christian.

20 pages

Here Is Your God - Dr. Robert A. Morey

Excerpts from **Battle Of The Gods**, a practical layman's guide on the nature and attributes of God. A must for every pastor, Sunday school teacher, and layperson.

142 pages

How To Keep Your Faith While In College

- Dr. Robert A. Morey

A survival manual for high school and college age students which gives the information they need to be faithful to the Lord during their college years. An excellent study guide with questions after each chapter. This book is an excellent gift idea for young people.

146 pages

How To Keep Your Kids Drug Free - Dr. Robert A. Morey

Christianity Today: "A brief convincing argument from Scripture against the use of drugs. It also contains practical counseling advice for teachers, pastors, and parents of drug abusers."

106 Pages

Introduction To Defending The Faith - Dr. Robert A. Morey

Noting that **all** Christians are called upon to defend the faith, Dr. Morey makes clear the principles and attitudes basic to that task, as they are expressed in a world-and-life view.

46 pages

The New Atheism and the Erosion of Freedom - Dr. Robert A. Morey

Dr James Kennedy: "Atheism has today become a force which Chirstians must take with the utmost seriousness."

176 pages

Reincarnation And Christianity - Dr. Robert A. Morey

If you read this book you will have the answers the next time the subject comes up!

Today over sixty million Americans accept reincarnation as a possibility. Among them are thousands of people who associate themselves with some branch of the Christian Church. Dr. Morey has undertaken the exploration, historical investigation and refutation of reincarnation.
60 Pages

Where Does It Say That - Bob Whitte

In the pages of this volume, the reader will find a wealth of information taken almost exclusively from primary Mormon historical sources. There are almost 200 actual photo-reprints, dozens of additional sources cited as well as special helps for the person trying to examine the claims of Mormonism.

Thus, the whole purpose for the existence of this volume is to make actual photo-copies of these original documents available to everyone. You now have at your fingertips, selected pages from several thousand dollars worth of rare books, pamphlets, diaries and manuscripts as well as companion quotations from many current Mormon sources. Use them well in your search for truth!
90 Pages

Behind the Watchtower Curtain - David Reed

This excellent book was written to answer claims made by the Watchtower organization, expose the false teaching, cultic practices, and to lay bare the secrets of the Watchtower organization. This book is a must reading for the potential convert, concerned relative, or concerned friend of anyone being lured into the Jehovah's Witnesses.
149 pages

Teaching / Ministry Helps Series - Dr. Richard P. Belcher

8 volumes of concise and helpful material for the teaching and preaching of the various Biblical books, including a teachable / preachable outline of the entire book, and expositional notes in a usable format.

1.) **Teaching Helps in I Peter**, 76 pages
2.) **Teaching Helps in Malachi**, 38 pages
3.) **Teaching Helps in II Corinthians**, 38 pages
4.) **Teaching Helps in Hebrews**, 56 pages
5.) **Teaching Helps in James**, 64 pages
6.) **Teaching Helps in Psalms** (A doctrinal approach to the book of Psalms), 53 pages
7.) **Ministry Helps in John**, 60 pages
8.) **Ministry Helps in Acts**, *** Due in May**

Preaching the Gospel - A Personal Method

by Dr. Richard P. Belcher

This is a book that will help not only the preacher who is beginning his ministry who wishes to build proper habits, but it will give aide also to the experienced preacher who wishes to improve his skills.
61 pages

Preaching the Gospel - A Theological Perspective by Dr. Richard P. Belcher

Using I Corinthians 1-4 and II Timothy 3:1-4:4 as the basis of study, Dr. Belcher sets forth the nature of the gospel we must preach and the nature of the methods we must employ. He argues we are not free to establish the nature or content of the gospel, neither are we free to determine the method of presentation. Clearly the presentation must be consistent with the grace and mystery nature of the gospel. Failure to understand this is what had led to the modern day demise of Biblical teaching.
58 pages

A Practical Approach to the Greek New Testament by Dr. Richard P. Belcher

An introduction to a practical use of the Greek NT helpful and useful for both those who have had Greek and those who have not.
52 pages

Diagramming the Greek New Testament
by Dr. Richard P. Belcher
A self-teaching manual whereby those who have some familiarity with the Greek NT can now learn to diagram it.
62 pages

Doing Biblical Exegesis by Dr. Richard P. Belcher
A manual which traces the basic steps in doing Biblical Exegesis in a minor or a major manner.
10 pages

Doing Textual Criticism in the Greek NT
by Dr. Richard P. Belcher
A manual which seeks to explain in a simple and understandable way the principles and practice of textual criticism in the Greek NT.
25 pages

Doing an Effective Greek Word Study by Dr. Richard P. Belcher
A manual which seeks to chart the procedure and sources for doing a Greek word study.
23 pages